Provost
Anthropology

Catalog
of
Fossil Hominids
of
North America

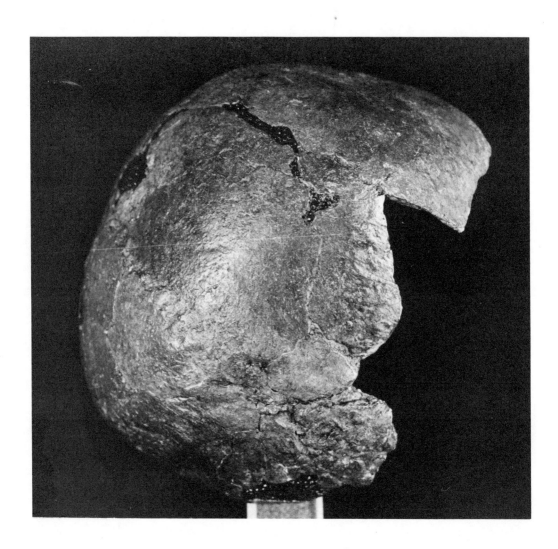

Plate 1. Los Angeles Man/Woman

Catalog
of
Fossil Hominids
of
North America

Reiner R. R. Protsch

Gustav Fischer New York • Stuttgart 1978

Reiner R. R. Protsch
Paleoanthropology and Archeometry
J. W. Goethe University (FB-16)

D-6000 Frankfurt/Main
Siesmayerstr. 70
West Germany

Library of Congress Cataloging in Publication Data

Protsch, Reiner R   R   1939-
    Catalog of fossil hominids of North America.

    Includes bibliographical references and index.
    1. Fossil man—North America. I. Title.
E71.P76   569'.9   78-12856
ISBN 0-89574-102-4

Printed in the United States of America.

ISBN 0-89574-102-4 Gustav Fischer New York
ISBN 3-437-10554-X Gustav Fischer Stuttgart

This work is dedicated to

Professor Dr. G. Kurth

on the occasion of his sixty-fifth birthday
honoring his more than forty years of contributions to the study of Anthropology and
Human Biology as well as other related
fields.

Preface

In 1936, W. and A. Quenstedt published the first catalog of fossil hominids (Fossilium Catalogus, Pars 74, Hominidae fossiles, Dr. W. Junk, Verlag für Naturwissenschaften, 's-Gravenhage) which was followed a year later by the catalog of E. Hue (Crânes paléolithiques. Bibliographie, in: Congrès préhistorique de France, XIIe session, Toulouse-Foix, 1936, pp. 113-285, Publication de la Société française, Paris) and was succeeded in 1953 by that of Vallois, Movius and Balout (Les Préhominiens et les hommes fossiles, Section V, Catalogue des hommes fossiles, XIX Congrès Géologique International, Alger 1953).

In more recent years, M. Day's *Guide to Fossil Man* (The Camelot Press Ltd., London, 1965, 287 pages) and T.W. Phenice's *Illustrated Key* (Hominid Fossils, Wm. C. Brown Co. Publishers, Dubuque, Iowa, 1972) attempted a more detailed coverage of the subject, but it was not until K.P. Oakley and B.G. Campbell published their catalog in 1967 (Catalogue of Fossil Hominids, Part I: Africa, Trustees of the British Museum of Natural History, London) that all Pleistocene fossil hominids of all continents were covered. The latter catalog was enlarged (Part II: Europe, 1971, with T.I. Molleson, and Part III: Americas, Asia, Australia, 1975) and is constantly revised as new finds come to the fore.

These catalogs, however, do not list those finds belonging to the early and middle Holocene, and therefore the need arose for a catalog with a more comprehensive listing of finds in the Americas, dating to more recent times than 10,000 years B.P. (before present). This catalog is purposely styled after Oakley and Campbell, because their outline is organized in such a way as to provide the student and specialist with the most detailed information on the subject. Their advice and help as well as their permission to use their format played an important part in the construction of this catalog.

I wish to thank Larry Mai for his invaluable help in the initial phases of the construction of this catalog. I am also thankful for the preparation of the typescript by Mrs. E. Richter, as well as to my wife who was helpful in arranging and proofreading this catalog.

Parts of the research were supported by the German National Science Foundation (Deutsche Forschungsgemeinschaft) through grants DFG Pr 143/1 and DFG Pr 143/3.

Contents

Introduction 1

    The Appearance of Anatomically Modern Man in the Americas 3

    Format of Catalog 7

The United States of America 9

    Angeles Mesa (Haverty Man) 11

    Arlington Springs 12

    Browns Valley 13

    Buena Vista Lake 14

    Burlington County 16

    Calaveras 17

    Capay 19

    Cimarron River (Folsom Man) 21

    Clear Fork (J.C. Putnam) 22

    Conkling Cavern 23

    Faulkner 25

    Gordon Creek 26

    Kawumkan Springs 27

    La Brea 29

    Lagow Sand Pit 31

    Laguna Beach 33

    Linger 35

    Little Sycamore 36

    Los Angeles 37

    Marmes 39

    McKean 41

    Medicine Crow 42

    Melbourne 43

    Midland 45

    Minnesota 47

    Mulberry Creek 48

    Natchez 50

    Nebraska ''Loess Man'' (Gilder Mound) 52

    Renier 54

Rock Bluff 55
Riverview Cemetary 56
Sauk Valley 57
Scripps Estates (La Jolla) (San Diego Man) 59
Stanford 61
Tecolote Point 62
Torrington 64
Tranquillity 65
Trenton 67
Utah Lake 68
Vero Beach 69
Worchester County 71
Yuha (Salton Sea) 72
Canada 75
Taber 77
Laguna Beach Woman 79
Map of North American Sites 80
Key to Map Locations 81
Index 83

INTRODUCTION

THE APPEARANCE OF ANATOMICALLY MODERN MAN IN THE AMERICAS

The question of the first appearance of "anatomically modern man" in the Americas has been a long and exhaustively debated point in paleoanthropology and archeology.

There are three basic problems that should be considered before an *ad hoc* acceptance of recent dating of some very early hominid remains is taken as a chronological marker for man's appearance on that continent.

1. Only one subspecies of *Homo sapiens* has occupied, at any given time, the American continent.
2. The most likely valid migrational route into the Americas, that is its two subcontinents, is from Asia.
3. The time of first appearance of subspecies of anatomically modern man in America and his successors the Indianoids and whether they are indeed related to Mongoloids is still uncertain.

It is proven that no other genus and species but *Homo sapiens* and only one subspecies, *Homo sapiens americanus*, ever has occupied the Americas (Blumenbach, 1775). Fossil subspecies of *Homo sapiens* such as *Homo sapiens neanderthalensis* or others, never have existed, nor have any other remains ever been found, on this continent. We can assume, therefore, that the only member of the family Hominidae in the Americas is a subspecies of "anatomically modern man," specifically the geographic subspecies *Homo sapiens americanus* (Blumenbach 1775). It should be pointed out that the name *Homo sapiens americanus* merely designates one of the many different varieties of *Homo sapiens* in its specific geographic setting. The term is not meant to designate racial characteristics but to designate a name to "anatomically modern man" on this continent. At a time period prior to 30,000 years B.P. the subspecies of *Homo sapiens* present on all continents are overall morphologically the same. Other such members are in Europe *Homo sapiens sapiens*, in Asia *Homo sapiens asiaticus*, in Australia *Homo sapiens australasicus*, as well as *Homo sapiens afer* in Africa. Early representatives of this basic "anatomically modern man" probably appeared on each continent between 40,000 and 30,000 years B.P. possibly after migration from Africa. Extensive dating by radiocarbon and supportive relative dating techniques, such as amino acid dating and microanalysis (F.U.N.), prove that a subspecies called *Homo sapiens capensis* formed in Africa the basis to all of the above mentioned geographic subspecies and originated possibly as early as 90,000 to 80,000 years B.P. (Protsch 1975).

The second problem is the possible migrational route taken by early immigrants into the Americas. It seems without doubt that the most suitable route is across the Bering Strait. A heated controversy, however, surrounds the time period during which immigration into the Americas can have occurred. A number of estimates exist as to when this land bridge could have been crossed, ranging anywhere from 100,000 to 10,000 years ago. These estimates are entirely "relative" geologic estimates and have at the present time no "absolute dating" supporting them. Most recent estimates (Butzer 1973) consider a land connection between the continents of Asia and America during the Altonian. There are several possibilities: one is from 60,000 to 30,000 years ago; others range from 25,000 to 15,000 and from 13,000 to 11,000 years B.P. A crossing of the strait during the latter periods into central and north Alaska was possible because they were free of ice; therefore further migration into the North American subcontinent was also possible along the area of the Mackenzie River. The latter route was closed during the period between 14,000 and 20,000 years B.P. All these hypotheses would be valid in connection with a theory of crossing if early "anatomically modern man" needed a land bridge for migration and if no other crossing other than by foot occurred.

Once migration had advanced beyond the ice- and snow-covered areas of North America a rapid infiltration into the two American Subcontinents could have occurred. That is to say, it is possible that within 5,000 years of his entering the American continent, man could have arrived at the most southern tip of South America.

The origin of Indians or Indianoids of the American Continent is claimed by numerous specialists to be closely linked to that of Mongoloids. This is based on a superficial similarity of morphologic characters, some of which are shared by man in Asia and the Americas. Ninety-five percent of early North American hominid remains which are relatively estimated to date from 10,000 years B.P. to about 2,000 years B.P. do indeed show many morphologic characteristics that are not too different from those characteristics seen in Mongoloids. Those remains, however, which date relatively as well as absolutely older than 10,000 years B.P. show morphologic features that separate them clearly from Mongoloids. A more extensive morphologic study of Laguna Beach Woman and Los Angeles Woman (not man) (Plhak 1975, 1977) indicate that these specimens are more closely aligned to what may be referred to as a "basic anatomically modern man" or what is by some specialists also called "archaic-caucasoid." The latter term seems on first glance to designate a racial category for these early American remains; however, it is merely meant to point out their morphologic similarity to very early specimens of "anatomically modern man" in Europe at around 30,000 years B.P. It is based on the assumption of many specialists that fossil specimens of earliest "anatomically modern man" are the same as those found in Europe, *Homo sapiens sapiens*, and that they are the earliest representatives of any subspecies of *Homo sapiens* anywhere in the world.

Within progressively more recent time periods, however, from about 10,000 years to 2,000 years B.P., typical Mongoloid features become more prominent in hominid remains found in the New World. There is also some indication of a geographic gradient of these features; the further north in America one goes the more apparently these features become pronounced.

This could be linked to the following hypothesis. Migration of a "basic anatomically modern man" occurred out of Africa around 40,000 to 35,000 years B.P. and the arrival of members of this group and migration into the different continents took place only a few thousand years later. After a few thousand years, each one of these "basic anatomically modern men" developed their own racial characteristics on the continents into which they had migrated; however, the typical racial features of each of the present-day races developed in response to different environmental pressures at different time periods. The Bushman Rock Shelter mandible (Protsch and De Villiers 1975), for example, seems to indicate that negroids had already developed around 29,500 years B.P. in Africa. In Europe, Asia, and other continents typical "racial features" developed at different times and somewhat later than those of negroids in Africa. The above reasoning is also strengthened by findings indicating that typical Mongoloid features are not found in "anatomically modern man" in Asia prior to 18,000 years B.P.

If this were true it would mean that early members of *Homo sapiens* showed the first racial features of any subspecies in America and also that "basic anatomically modern man" developed in America, not in Africa or Europe. These dates, going back to earlier than 35,000 years B.P., are quite peculiar because earliest "anatomically modern man" dates in Europe to not earlier than 32,000 to 34,000 years B.P., in Australia to ca. 34,000 years B.P., and in Asia to around the same time. An exception is Africa, with dates on "basic anatomically modern man" to prior to 60,000 years B.P.

To summarize the above we can say that everybody agrees that no remains of any other fossil hominid, such as Neanderthal or *Homo erectus*, have ever been found in America prior to "anatomically modern man" and that finds of fossil hominids other than modern man are necessary before even a theory of development of early Americans, i.e., "anatomically modern man," from such fossil predecessors can be stated. Dates earlier than 35,000 years B.P. in the Americas therefore must be faulty.

All hominid finds belonging to "anatomically modern man" cannot date earlier than 35,000 to 30,000 years B.P. and are merely manifestations of a population that has migrated into America at around that time and that has developed racial features unique to the American Indian down to 10,000 to 8,000 years B.P. Subsequent migrations at more recent times have brought Mongoloid characteristics from Asia into the Americas and these features can be clearly seen in some Indian tribes of North America and in the Eskimos.

References

Bada, J.L., Schroeder, R.A., and Carter, G.F. (1974). New Evidence for the Antiquity of Man in North America deduced from Aspartic Acid Racemization. *Science* 184:791–793.

Bada, J.L., and Helfman, P. (1977). "Evidence for a 50,000 year Antiquity for Man in the America Derived from the Amino Acid Racemization Analysis of Human Skeletons." Lecture given at the SWAA Congress in San Diego, California, on the 7th of April 1977.

Blumenbach, J.F. (1775). "De generis humani varietate nativa." Ph.D. Dissertation, Göttingen University.

Butzer, K.W. (1973). *Environment and Archaeology. An ecological approach to prehistory.* 2nd. Ed. Chicago, New York: Aldine-Atheron.

Plhak, M. (1975). "Chronologie und Morphologie der ältesten fossilen Hominiden Amerikas." Diplomarbeit (Masters Thesis), Fachbereich Biologie, Anthropologie, J.W. Goethe Universität, Frankfurt/Main, W. Germany.

Plhak, M. (1977). Die Morphologie der fossilen Hominiden von Laguna Beach und Los Angeles. Zeits. fur Anthropol. Morphol., 1978, in press.

Protsch, R. (1975) The Absolute Dating of Upper Pleistocene SubSaharan Fossil Hominids and Their Place in Human Evolution. *J. Human Evol.* 4:297–322.

Protsch, R., and De Villiers, H. (1975). Bushman Rock Shelter, Origstad, Eastern Transvaal, South Africa: Chronology and Morphology of a childs mandible. *J. Human Evol.* 3:387–396.

FORMAT OF CATALOG

Each numbered entry contains the following information in the order (adapted from Oakley and Campbell, 1967).

1. The geographic location nearest to the site after which the hominid remains are named; date of find if more than one find has occurred at the same site.
2. The location of the site in terms of (a) direction and distance from a population or other center easily found on a map. and/or (b) map quadrant and/or longitude and latitude.
3. Discoverer and date of discovery; excavation supervisor(s) and date of excavation.
4. The stratigraphic context in which the remains have been discovered (or soil profile).
5. Whether or not the remains appear to be a burial.
6. Geologic age of formation in which remains are situated at time of discovery.
7. Archeologic artifacts associated with remains; cultural affiliation.
8. Flora or fauna associated with remains.
9. Microanalysis (F,U,N).
10. Absolute data:
   A1: based on ^{14}C date (or such other absolute/relative dates as amino acid dating) of residual bone collagen or other organic tissue/human remains.
   A2: based on ^{14}C date of organic matter directly associated with human remains.
   A3: based on ^{14}C date of organic matter from another site culturally contemporaneous with site of human remains.
11. Brief description of remains.
12. First report of remains/site.
13. First publication of exhaustive anatomic description of human remains.
14. Recent revision of literature.
15. Location of photographs (in literature).
16. Other relevant publications.
17. Location of remains today; catalogue number.
18. Location of manufacturer of casts, if available.

THE UNITED STATES OF AMERICA

ANGELES MESA (HAVERTY MAN)

1. Angeles Mesa (Haverty Man).
2. 438 m West of Angeles Mesa Drive, 275 m South of railroad tracks, on the Spanish land grant called Paso de la Tijera (Santa Monica Quadrangle, USGS), between Los Angeles and Culver City, California.
3. By the Thomas Haverty Co. in March 1924; investigated by William Alanson Bryan 1924.
4. Locality 1 sequence of deposits: a conformable sequence, ". . . consisting largely of drab or olive colored, unconsolidated, micaceous sands and sandy clays . . . the bed in which the human remains were found lies below the narrow third dark band and above a clay . . . with some carbonaceous matter. Below this is a greenish micaceous sand." Found 48–58 cm deep in alluvial soil, in an open area drained by Ballona Creek, in a 30-cm^2 area (until recently a pond and marsh environment) (Stock 1924).
5. Six burials, some in normal articulation.
6. Undetermined (Early Holocene?).
7. A quartzite boulder, regarded as an implement, and a small awl-like object were recovered.
8. Recent mollusks (Stock 1924).
9. ———
10. ———
11. Angeles Mesa 1–6. Five adults: "a sixth individual somewhat younger, may be a female." Somewhat mineralized.
12. Stock, Chester (1924). A recent discovery of ancient human remains in Los Angeles, California. *Science* n.s., 60(1540):2–5.
13. ———
14. ———
15. ———
16. Merriam, J.C. (1924). Present status of investigations concerning the antiquity of Man in California. *Science* n.s., 60(1540):1–2.
    Wallace, J.W. (1955). A suggested chronology for southern California coastal archaeology. *Southwest J. Anthropol.* 11(3):214–230.
17. Los Angeles Museum of Natural History, Los Angeles, California.
18. ———

ARLINGTON SPRINGS

1. Arlington Springs.
2. Exposure on W side of Arlington Canyon 400 m (1/4 mile) from beach, Santa Rosa Island, California. 34°00'N, 120°10'W.
3. P.C. Orr in 1959. Discovery was investigated by geologists and archaeologists in 1960.
4. At 11 m (37 ft) in alluvial sediments (Tecolote member). Orr, P.C. (1962). The Arlington Spring site, Santa Rosa Island, California, *Am. Antiq.* 27:417–419.
5. No evidence of burial.
6. End Pleistocene, Late Wisconsin.
7. No artifacts.
8. *Peromyscus*, marine Mollusca.
9. Human femur: $F = 1.2\%$ $100F/P205 = 3.6$, $eU308 = 28$ ppm, $N = 0.23\%$, (No associated animal bone has yet been sent for analysis by P.C. Orr.) Oakley, K.P. (1963), Relative dating of Arlington Springs Man, *Science*, 141:1172.
10. A2: $10,000 \pm 200$ B.P. on basis of radiocarbon in associated charcoal in rich organic band (L 650). Olson, E.A. and Broecker, W.S. (1961). Lamont natural radiocarbon measurements VII, *Radiocarbon* 3:170–171.
    A1: Berger, R., Orr, P.C., and Protsch, R., In preparation.
11. Arlington Springs 1. Adult: 2 femora (f) and postcranial fragment.
12. Orr, P.C. (1960). Late Pleistocene marine terraces on Santa Rosa Island, California, *Bull. Geol. Soc. Am.* 71:1113–1120.
13. ———
14. ———
15. ———
16. Orr, P.C. (1962). Arlington Springs Man, *Science* 135:219.
17. Santa Barbara Museum, Natural History, Santa Barbara, California.
18. ———

BROWNS VALLEY

1. Browns Valley.
2. Gravel pit, traverse count, 60 miles SW of Fergus Falls, Minnesota. 45° 45′ N, 96° 45′ W.
3. H. Jensen in 1933. Investigated by A.E. Jenks, University of Minnesota 1935.
4. Intrusive pit in gravel. Jenks, A.E. (1937), Minnesota's Browns Valley Man and associated burial artifacts, *Mem. Am. Anthropal Assoc.* 49, Menasha, Wisconsin.
5. Burial, presumably from the surface of the gravel, soon after its deposition; pit covered with undisturbed humus layer.
6. Terminal Pleistocene/Early Holocene. Leverett, F., and Sardeson F.W. Quaternary geology of Minnesota and parts of adjacent states, *Prof. Pap. U.S. Geol. Surv.*, 161:119–146. Jenks, A.E. (1937).
7. Paleo-Indian. Associated flaked lanceolate projectile points and sandstone abraders.
8. ——
9. ——
10. A3: Projectile points of the associated type ca. 8,500 B.P. (*fide* H.T. Irwin, Washington State University, Pullman).
11. Browns Valley 1. "Browns Valley Man." Male, 28–40 years old: cranium (f), mandibula, all but 5 dentes present.
12. Jenks, A.E. (1937).
13. Jenks (1937). Fairly dolichocephalic, leptorrhine type; North American Indian.
14. ——
15. Jenks (1937).
16. A. Hrdlicka (1937). The "Minnesota Man". *Am. J. Phys. Anthropol.* 22:175–199.
17. Owned by the estate of W.H. Jenson, Browns Valley, Minnesota.
18. ——

BUENA VISTA LAKE

1. Buena Vista Lake.
2. Open alluvial site (Site 2) on the SW edge of Buena Vista Lake at the foot of the Buena Vista Hills, between Taft and Bakersfield (Buena Vista Quadrangle), in the San Joaquin Valley; in the N half of the SE quarter of the NE quarter of Sec. 1, Twp. 32S, Range 24E.
3. Historical village of Tulamni called "Tulaminu" (or Tulamni place); excavated by E.F. Walker and Waldo F. Wedel in 1933–1934.
4. Alluvial flat and sandspit between lakeshore and low hills; at 15–25 cm in the deepest level of human occupation, the so-called "plum-pudding" — yellow compact sand, gravel, and some shell mixed with alluvium washed down from the hills; the "plum-pudding" overlays the Tulare formation soil zone (Wedel 1941).
5. Four interments, all extended. Nos. 17 and 18 shared a common grave with 193 cm in depth, both prone; No. 28 with 203 cm depth, supine; No. 40 with 257 cm depth supine. All lime encrusted, No. 40 badly decomposed.
6. Holocene.
7. Paleo-Indian or Archaic; yellow ochre pigment, 4 mullers, 1 "crude" leaf-shaped, unstemmed, chipped point.
8. ———
9. ———
10. ———
11. Buena Vista Lake 17. Subadult: skeletal remains.
    18. Adult, female: skeletal remains.
    28. Skeletal remains.
    40. Skeletal remains.
12. Wedel, Waldo R. (1941). *Archaeological Investigations at Buena Vista Lake, Kern County, California*. Bulletin 130. Washington, D.C.: U.S. Bureau of American Ethnology.
13. Stewart, T. Dale (1941). Skeletal remains from the Buena Vista Lake sites, California. Appendix A *in* Wedel (1941).

14. ———
15. Wedel (1941).
16. ———
17. United States National Museum, Washington, D.C.
18. ———

BURLINGTON COUNTY

1. Burlington County.
2. " . . . in a field near a small settlement known as Sykesville. It had rolled out of the bank of a brook running through the field." Near Trenton, New Jersey.
3. Anonymous 1879.
4. In the "southern drift," as the white pebbles and yellow sand are called, beneath a "rich alluvial deposit" (Hrdlicka 1907).
5. ——
6. Unknown (probably Recent).
7. ——
8. ——
9. ——
10. ——
11. Burlington County 1. Female adult: calvaria (chamoecephalic).
12. Anon. (?) (1902). *Bull. Am. Mus. Nat. Hist.* 16.
13. Anon. (1902).
14. Hrdlicka, Ales (1907). *Skeletal remains suggesting or attributed to early man in North America.* Bulletin 33. Washington, D.C.: U.S. Bureau of American Ethnology. Similar to chamoecephalic skulls of Bremen, Germany; not Indian.
15. Hrdlicka (1907).
16. Bibliography in item 12.
17. Peabody Museum, Harvard University, Cambridge, Massachusetts. Cat. No. 19513.
18. ——

CALAVERAS

In 1866 a gold miner named Mattison found a stalagmite-encrusted lump at 130 ft (39.6 m) in gravel of early Pliocene age in his mine at Table Mountain in Calaveras county, California. The specimen was investigated by J.D. Whitney, State Geologist of California, who found that the calcareous crust covered the vault and facial bones of a human skull. Its antiquity long remained controversial. Chemical analyses made in 1879 of the skull and of Pliocene rhinoceros bone from the Calaveras gravel revealed considerable differences. The rhinoceros bone contained 4.77% calcium fluoride, whereas none was recorded in the analysis of the human skull, indicating that a large proportion of the bone had been replaced by calcium carbonate. In the collection of the United States National Museum, Hrdlicka found two comparatively recent skulls (Reg. Nos. USNM 225.171 and 225.172) preserved in the same way with an incrustation of stalagmite which had been collected from old caves in Calaveras county. The Calaveras skull had possibly been derived originally from the same source, but if so, it had been placed fraudulently in the gold mine. Calaveras skull (Harvard No. 97-40-10/N74963): F = 0.22%, 100 F/P205 = 2.2, eU308 = nil ppm, N = 0.63%. Calaveras cave skull (UNSM 225.172): F = 0.28%, 100F/P205 = 2.4, eU308 = nil ppm, N = 0.70%.

Rhinoceros antiquitatis (antique rhinoceros), Pliocene, Calaveras: F = 2.3% 100F/P205 = 10.3,* mammal bone, Pliocene (Hemphillian), Loc. V3212, Oakdale, Calaveras: F = 1.97%, 100F/P205 = 5.9, eU308 = ppm, N = n.d.

The skull is preserved in the Peabody Museum, Harvard University, Cambridge, Massachusetts, Reg. No. 97-40-10/N74963.

Holmes, W.H. (1899). A Review of the evidence relating to the Auriferous Gravel Man in California. *Rep. Smithsonian Inst.* 1899:419–472.

Hrdlicka, A. (1907). Skeletal remains suggesting or attributed to early man, *Smithsonian Inst. Bur. Ethnol.* 33:21–28.

Vayson, A. (1932), de Pradenne, *Les Fraudes Archéologie Préhistorique,* Paris: Colin, A. p. 142, footnote.

Whitney, J.D. (1879). The auriferous gravels of the Sierra Nevada of California, *Mem. Harvard Mus. Comp. Anat.* 6:258–288.

*Recalculation of analysis made in 1879.

Wilson, T. (1902), La hauta ancienneté de l'homme dans l'amerique du Nord, *C.R. Congr. Int. Anthrop. Arch. Préhist.,* Paris (XIIe sess., 1900):158–170.

Notes contributed by K.P. Oakley

CAPAY

1. Capay.
2. A stream bank in Cobbey Canyon, about 3 miles S of the town of Guinda in Yolo County; the location is in the SW quarter of the NW quarter of Sec. 22, of Twp. 11N, Range 3W, M.D.B. and M. The Rumsey Quadrangle, USGS. The site has been designated by the UCAS as Yol-2. California.
3. W.F. Yerington in November 1950; investigated by M. Baumhoff, R.F. Heizer, and F. Harradine in 1951.
4. Embedded in a small, dome-shaped, softly consolidated and calcareous Pliocene substratum formation comprised of nonmarine sediments. An upper, superficial layer is a dark soil, identified as Zamora loam; the depth of this layer is 102 cm. The articulated burial was placed in a grave dug from a point not higher than the light brown calcareous deposit, so that the maximum depth of the grave may be calculated at about 76 cm. The bones then lay at a depth of 178 cm from the surface at the time of discovery. (Heizer and Cook 1953).
5. Articulated, loosely flexed burial.
6. Holocene; about 2,000 B.P. (Harradine 1953), about 4,000 B.P. (Heizer and Cook 1953).
7. No artifacts reported.
8. None reported.
9. Human remains: percent of weight of bone: $Ca = 33.4$, $P = 15.7$, $Co_2 = 7.62$, ash weight (ignition loss) $= 6.39$, $C = 2.08$; Older than Middle Culture sites Sac-43, CCO-137, and Sac-151 and younger than the Early Culture sites LAn-1, Sac-107, SJO-142, and Fre-48. The figures for total organic matter, carbon, and also water content, are closest to those for sites SJo-68 and SBa-7.
10. ———
11. Capay 1. "Capay Man" adult male: skull "with some parts missing," and mention of skeletal remains in articulation; dolichocephalic.
12. Heizer, Robert F., and Cook, S.F. (1953). Capay Man, an ancient central California Indian burial. *Univ. Calif. Archaeol. Surv. Repts,* No. 22, paper 24, pp. 24–26.
13. ———
14. ———

15. Photographs on file at University of California at Berkeley but not reproduced in print.
16. Harradine, Frank (1953). Report on pedologic observations made at the "Capay Man" site in western Yolo County. *Univ. Calif. Archaeol. Surv. Repts,* No. 22, paper 25, p. 27.
17. Museum of Anthropology, University of California, Berkeley, California.
18. ———

CIMARRON RIVER (FOLSOM MAN)

1. Cimarron River (Folsom Man).
2. At a point on the Cimarron River 8 miles E of Folsom, New Mexico, ¾ mile SE of the junction of the Cimarron Canyon Highway and the road to Branson.
3. Found and removed by J.C. McKinley in January 1935; given to J.D. Figgins.
4. In the S bank of the Cimarron River, a reported 162 cm below the alluvial surface, in a lens of fine quartz sand and lime (Figgins 1935).
5. "Accidental disposition indicated" (Roberts 1937).
6. Conditions against an accurate date (Roberts 1937); possibly near Early Holocene.
7. ———
8. ———
9. ———
10. ———
11. Cimarron River 1. Male, middle aged: skull (f) (dolichocephalic), mandible; vertebrae (ff), "hand and arm bones," scapulae (ff), pelvis (f), tibiae (f), fibulae (f), femorae (f).
12. Figgins, J.D. (1935). New World Man. *Colorado Mus. Nat. Hist. Proc.,* 14(1): 1–5. Declared a new species, *Homo novus mundus Sp. Nov.,* because of "the unusual features. . .".
13. Figgins (1935).
14. Roberts, Frank H.H., Jr. (1937). New World Man. *Am. Antiq.* 2:172–177. Also *in* Roberts (1937): Ales Hrdlicka, Earnest A. Hooton, George Woodbury, and Harry L. Shapiro, all of whom agree that *"Homo novus mundus Sp. Nov."* falls within the range of *Homo sapiens,* especially early American Indian.
15. Roberts, (1937), plate 12.
16. ———
17. Denver Museum of Natural History, Denver, Colorado.
18. Denver Museum of Natural History, Denver, Colorado.

CLEAR FORK (J.C. PUTNAM)

1. Clear Fork (J.C. Putnam).
2. On the Clear Fork of the Brazos River, J.C. Putnam Ranch, 60 miles NE of Abilene, Texas.
3. Found by three boys in June 1943; investigated by Cyrus N. Ray in 1943.
4. Found 55 cm below alluvial valley floor, in the Elm Creek (or Nugent, according to source) silts, believed deposited during the pluvial period corresponding to the Wisconsin substage (Roberts, 1945).
5. Burial.
6. Terminal Pleistocene (Roberts, 1945).
7. ⎯⎯⎯
8. ⎯⎯⎯
9. ⎯⎯⎯
10. ⎯⎯⎯
11. Clear Fork 1. Male, about 40 years: incomplete cranium, mandible; 2 humeri, 2 radii, 2 ulnae, 2 femora, 2 tibiae, 2 fibulae, 2 innominates (f), 2 scapulae (f), 10 vertebrae (f), "and many of the smaller bones in good condition" (Stewart, 1945).
12. Ray, Cyrus N. (1943). Human burial covered by Twenty-one feet of silt. *Bull. Texas Archaeol. Paleontol. Soc.* No. 15:110–116. ⎯⎯ (1943). A Texas Skeleton. *Science 98(2546):344.*
13. Stewart, T. Dale (1945). Report on J.C. Putnam skeleton from Texas. *Bull. Texas Archaeol. Paleontol. Soc. Bull.* No. 16:31–40. Abilene.
14. Roberts, Frank H.H. Jr. (1945). A deep burial on the Clear Fork of the Brazos River. *Texas Archaeol. Paleontol. Soc.* No. 16:9–30, Abilene.
15. Stewart (1945).
16. Leighton, M.M. (n.d.) Geological aspects of the findings of primitive man near Abilene, Texas. (Preliminary Report). *Medallion Papers,* No. XXIV. Gila Pueblo, Globe, Arizona.
17. Division of Physical Anthropology, United States National Museum, Washington, D.C.
18. ⎯⎯⎯

CONKLING CAVERN

1. Conkling Cavern.
2. Cave on W edge of White Sands Military Reservation, at foot of Bishop's Cap mountain, in San Andres mountains (Orange Range) and due W of highest peak, near Las Cruces, New Mexico. 32°40'N, 106°40'W.
3. Cave found by local ranchers. Investigated by R.P. Conkling in 1929.
4. Cave deposit of reddish windblown sand, 6.1–9.7 m (20–32 ft) below surface which was sealed by flagstone floor; highest "burial" beneath sloth remains. Bryan, W.A. (1929). The recent bone-cavern find at Bishop's Cap, New Mexico, *Science,* 70:39–41 New York.
   Conkling, R.P. (1932). Conkling Cavern: The discoveries in the bone cave at Bishop's Cap, New Mexico, *Bull. Sul Ross St. Teach. Coll.* 44:6–19 *(Publ. W. Tex. Hist. Sci. Soc.,* No. 4.)
5. Burial site or natural trap.
6. Late Pleistocene/Early Holocene.
7. ———
8. *Nothrotherium,* formerly / *Nothrotheriops shastense* (ground sloth), *Equus occidentalis* (extinct horse), *Tanupolama sp.* (fossil camel), *Camelops hesternus* (fossil camel), *Megalonyx jeffersoni* (giant ground sloth) (Conkling 1932).
9. Human remains: mandibula, F = 0.10%, dens, F = 0.10%, humerus, F = 0.18%; ulna, F = 0.15%; *radius, F* = 0.47%; parietalia, F = 0.14%. Associated fauna: *Camelus,* F = 0.01%; *Megalonyx,* F = 0.07–0.99%. *Equus*, F = 0.03–0.07%. Stewart, T.D. (1952), The fluorine content of associated human and extinct animal bones from the Conkling Cavern, New Mexico. *Science,* 116:457–458 New York.
10. A1: 1,590 ± 80 B.P. (UCLA - 1059) on ^{14}C in collagen of human femur. Berger, R., and Libby, W.F. (1969), *UCLA Radiocarbon Dates IX,* 11:195–196. A1: 5,320 ± 120 B.P. (UCLA - 1432) on ^{14}C in collagen of human femur. Berger, R., and Libby, W.F. (1969), *Radiocarbon* 11:195–196. Berger, R., and Protsch, R. In preparation.
11. Conkling 1–4: Four scattered skeletons including 2 calottes (f), one with parietalia and frontale, the other with occipitale and temporale.
12. Bryan (1929).

13. Stewart, T.D. (1951). Preliminary observations on the human skeletal remains from Conkling Cavern, New Mexico. *Am. J. Phys. Anthropol.* 9:237 (abstract).

14. ———

15. ———

16. ———

17. Department of Paleontology, Los Angeles County Museum, Los Angeles, California, Reg. No. unknown. Paleo- Indian Institute, Eastern New Mexico University, Portales, New Mexico. Reg. No. unknown.

18. ———

FAULKNER

1. Faulkner.
2. Ohio River bottom land, SW quarter of the NW quarter of Sec. 24, Twp. 16S, Range 6E, Massac County, Illinois; site on land owned by Rev. Orange Faulkner.
3. Richard S. MacNeish in 1941; excavation led by MacNeish in 1944.
4. Zone C, stratified alluvial clay (MacNeish 1948).
5. "Eleven burials were uncovered during the excavation. Two were so fragmentary that they defy description as to the position of the skeletons. One was represented by only a skull. The skeletal material from the Faulkner site was fragmentary and almost completely deteriorated. Wet soil conditions added to the difficulty of locating and preserving bone" (MacNeish 1948, p. 236).
6. Holocene (Est: 6,000 B.P.).
7. Faulkner focus; Archaic pattern.
8. Fauna: undetermined long bone artifacts; flora: "charred hickory nuts" (MacNeish 1948, p. 239).
9. ——
10. ——
11. Faulkner 1–. Eleven skeletons (ff).
12. MacNeish, Richard S., (1948). The pre-pottery Faulkner site of southern Illinois. *Am. Antiq.* 13(3):232–243. Salt Lake City.
13. ——
14. ——
15. ——
16. ——
17. Museum of Anthropology, University of Michigan, Ann Arbor, Michigan.
18. ——

GORDON CREEK

1. Gordon Creek.
2. On small tributary of Gordon Creek, S of Roosevelt National Forest Boundary, Larimer County, Colorado, 43°43′20″N, 105°22′80″W. University of Colorado Museum Archaeological Survey designation 5LR99.
3. H. Wertzbaugh, U.S. Forest Service 1960. Investigated by D. Breternitz in 1963, and D.C. Anderson, University of Colorado in 1964.
4. "Alluvium" at a depth of 1,5 m below present surface Anderson, D.C. (1966). The Gordon Creek burial. *Southwestern Lore* 32: 1–9.
   —— (1967). Unpublished Field Notes, Hell Gap Expedition, Peabody Museum, Harvard University.
5. Pit Burial in a layer beneath a soil zone (Anderson, 1966).
6. Terminal Pleistocene/Early Holocene.
7. Paleo-Indian or Early Archaic (Anderson, 1966). Tools are described as undiagnostic but appear to be Paleo-Indian, probably the Agate Basin Complex.
8. Rodentia, unidentified micromammalia, *Cervus canadensis* (canadian deer) (Anderson, 1966). Two worked animal ribs and 4 elk teeth.
9. ——
10. A1: 9,700 ± 250 B.P. (7,750 B.C.) on basis of ^{14}C dating of collagen fraction of left ilium (GX-0530); carbonate fraction 3,540 ± 130 B.P. (Anderson, 1966).
11. Gordon Greek 1. Male, 25–30' years: cranium (?), mandibula, l. humerus, l. radius, l. ulna, vertebrae, l. os coxae, tibia, fibula (for complete list see Breternitz *et al*. 1971).
12. Anderson (1966).
13. Complete: Breternitz *et al*. (1962). Excavations at three sites in the Verde Valley, Arizona. *Am. Antiq.* 28 (2):251–252.
    Breternitz, D.A., Swedlund, A.C., and Anderson, D.C. (1971). An early burial from Gordon Creek, Colorado. *Am. Antiq.* 36(2):170–182.
14. Breternitz, David A., Swedlund, Alan C., and Anderson, Duane C., (1971), An early burial from Gordon Creek, Colorado. *Am. Antiq.* 36:170–182.
15. ——
16. ——
17. University of Colorado Museum, Boulder, Colorado.
18. ——

KAWUMKAN SPRINGS

1. Kawumkan Springs.
2. The Kawumkan Springs Midden lies in the SE quarter of the SE quarter, Twp. 34S, Range 8E, Williamette Meridian, on the Klamath Indian Reservation, Oregon; approximately 42°35'N, 121°42'W, in the roughly rectangular area formed by the Kawumkan Springs on the south, the Sprague River on the east, the low ridge of exposed scoriacious basalt on the west, and the open meadow below the timber on the north.
3. Historic house pits built on kitchen midden; excavated in 1948–1951 by L.S. Cressman.
4. Open site kitchen midden averaging 1–2 m in depth, arealy 30– by 75m, resting on a badly disintegrated sandstone.
5. Thirteen burials from levels III–IV.
6. Holocene (6,453 ± 250 B.P., C-247).
7. Levels III–IV are lower Klamath Lake Early Horizon. ''The most important bone specimen is the long bone projectile point with the bevelled end for hafting to a shaft. This was found in the lower left abdominal part of the skeleton, 11-222, buried in the 'kitchen' . . . . This point is exactly like those described from the Early Horizon at Lower Klamath Lake (Cressman, 1942). (Also found was a) side-notched projectile point in the skull of this skeleton. These bevelled bone points are known from the Clovis horizon where they occur with the Clovis fluted points (Sellards Llano Culture), . . . In view of the Lower Klamath Lake area of use and the horizon represented here, it is clear that in the present state of our information this burial must be associated with that horizon. This association not only dates the specimen but the 'kitchen' in which this victim of attack was buried'' (Cressman, 1956, pp. 431–432).
8. Avifauna: 3 kinds of ducks (20-776, 20-780, 20-838), *Xanthocephalus xanthocephalus* (yellow-headed blackbird, 20-847); Pisces misc. vertebrae and sucker, *Gila, Siphateles,* Salmonidae (salmons), (trout? 20-820, 20-624).
9. ———
10. A2: 6,450 ± 250 B.P. (C-247) from a tree killed by the eruption of Mount Mazama. Pumice and ash dating from this eruption was found in the lower strata of level III. Level IV commences at about 7,500 B.P. (Cressman 1956, chart 3, p. 464).

11. Kawumkan Springs 1–13 (from levels III–IV):
  KS 1. (11-220): crushed, no description.
  KS 2. (11-221): adult, 40–50 years; calvaria, rt. femur (f), lt. femur (f), rt humerus (ff).
  KS 3. (11-222): adult, 25–35 years; calvaria, maxilla (f) but with 16 teeth, mandible with 7 teeth, portions of the long bones and pelvis.
  KS 4. (11-223): nuchal, temporal portion of the skull.
  KS 5. (11-224): subadult, 12 years: mandible lacking rami, rt. femur (f), rt. ilium (f), rt. mastoid (f).
  KS 6. (11-225): portion of adolescent cranium.
  KS 7. (11-226): young adult: 2 parietal, 2 temporal, 1 lambdoid, plus sections of long bones.
  KS 8. (11-232): portions of long bones.
  KS 9. (11-233): fragment of lt. femur.
  KS 10. (11-234): 2 femora.
  KS 11. (11-235): male: frontal (f), lt. parietal (f), occipital (f), lt. mastoid (f), mandible (ff), lt. femur (f), lt. humerus (f).
  KS 12. (11-236): female, young adult: complete skeleton.
  KS 13. (11-237): small fragments of cranium (used for test of $CaCO_3$ as mineralizing material).
12. Cressman, L.S. (1956). Klamath prehistory. *Trans. Am. Phil. Soc.* n. s., 46:pt. 4. Philadelphia.
13. Laughlin, William S. (1956). Appendix C *in* Cressman (1956).
14. ———
15. Cressman, L.S. (1956). n.s. Klamath Prehistory. *Trans. Am. Phil. Soc.* n.s., 46:pt. 4.
16. ———
17. Oregon State Museum of Anthropology, University of Oregon, Eugene, Oregon.
18. ———

LA BREA

1. La Brea.
2. Rancho La Brea asphalt deposits, pit 10, immediately to the North of the Los Angeles Museum of Art, Wilshire Blvd. Los Angeles *Co,* California, Feb. 5, 1914, under direction of Frank S. Daggett.
3. ———
4. Pit 10: see Merriam (1914). Stock (1946), pp. 24–26. In the north of two vents or chimenys filled with asphalt; depth of 15–23 cm.
5. No burial; intrusive into natural asphalt.
6. ———
7. ———
8. Merriam (1914): *Teratornis merriami* (condor), *Equus occidentalis* (extinct horse).
9. Merriam (1914).
10. A1: 9,000 ± 80 B.P. (UCLA 1292 bb). A3: 4,450 ± 250 B.P. Howard, Hildegarde (1960). Significance of carbon-14 dates for Rancho La Brea. *Science* 131 (3402):712–714. Washington, D.C.
11. Rancho La Brea 1. Young female: cranium and mandibula, "some postcranial parts." Heizer, R.F. in Kroeber, Alfred L., 1962. The Rancho La Brea Skull. *Am. Antiq.* 27(3):416–417. Salt Lake City.
12. Merriam, J.C. (1914), Preliminary report on the discovery of human remains in an asphalt deposit at Rancho La Brea. *Science* 40(1023): 198–203. New York.
13. Merriam, J.C. (1914). Preliminary report on the discovery of human remains in an asphalt deposit at Rancho La Brea. *Science n.s., 40(1023):198–203.* New York.
14. Kroeber, A.L. (1962). The Rancho La Brea Skull, *Am. Antiq.* 27 (3):416. Berger, R., Protsch, Reiner, Reynolds, Richard, Rozaire, Charles, and Sackett, James R. (1971). New radiocarbon dates based on bone collagen of California paleo-Indians. *Contrib. Univ. Calif. Archaeol. Res. Fac.* Berkeley, No 12:43—49. Plhak, M. (1975). "Chronologie und Morphologie der frühesten fossilen Hominiden Amerikas." Masters Thesis, University of Frankfurt.
15. Kroeber (1962).
16. Hrdlicka, Ales (1918). *Recent Discoveries Attributed to Early Man in America.* Bulletin 66. Washington, D.C.: *Bureau of American Ethnology,* Hildegarde, H. and Miller, A.H. (1939). The avifauna associated with human remains at Rancho

La Brea, California. *Carnegie Insti. Washington, Publication 514, Paper 3,* pp. 39–48. Washington.

Stock, C. (1946). Rancho La Brea; a record of Pleistocene life in California. *Los Angeles County Museum, Science Series,* No. 11, *Paleontology* No. 7, Los Angeles.

17. Los Angeles County Museum of Natural History, Los Angeles, California.
18. ———

LAGOW SAND PIT

1. Lagow Sand Pit.
2. On the Trinity River (terrace), near Dallas, Texas.
3. By workmen on October 26, 1920; investigated by Ellis W. Shuler 1920–1922.
4. Found 13 cm below the present surface in a zone of fine sandy yellow clay (the Upper Shuler yellow sandy clays), probably intrusive into this subformation (Crook, 1961). Intrusion probably from the surface of the yellow clay, before the Richards alluvium subformation deposition.
5. "... it could even have been a burial" (Crook, 1961).
6. Terminal Pleistocene–Holocene.
7. ———
8. *Mammonteus americanus (M. primigenius?)* (mammoth), *Camelops hesternus* (fossil camel), *Bison antiquus figginsi* (bison), *Tetrameryx sp.* (extinct pronghorn antelope), *Cervus elaphus* (deer). (Crook and Harris 1952).
9. Data from Shuler (1923):

	$P_2O_5(\%)$	CaO	
		(ppm)	(%)
Human	30.0	57.8	32.3
Camel	31.5	55.4	31.04

"Actually, as we now know, neither the lime content nor the phosphate content necessarily changes in course of time." (Oakley and Howells (1961). Age of the skeleton from the Lagow sand pit, Texas. *Am. Antiq.* 26:543–545.) Data from Oakley, K.P., and Howells, W.W. (1961):

Specimen	Fluorine*	eU_3O_8 (ppm)	N(%)
Recent animal bone	3.34 (0.03%)	0	4.00
Human rib, Lagow	3.13	3	1.20
Human tibia, Lagow	3.12	0	1.20
Mammoth, Lagow	2.65	64	0.40
Camelops, Lagow	2.73	36	0.50
Tepexpan human skeleton	2.67 (1.5%)	1	0.06
Midland human skull	3.13 (0.70%)	13	0.03

*X-ray diffraction data. Difference in mm between $2_0(004)$ and $2_0(140)$ for Copper Koc radiation in 19-cm diameter powder camera.

The bones are intrusive and not directly associated with the mammoth and *Camelops* (Oakley and Howells 1961).

10. ———
11. Lagow Sand Pit 1. Male, adult (fragments of calotte). Two femora (f), 2 tibiae (f), rt. fibula (f), lt. horizontal ramus of mandible.
12. Shuler, E.W. (1923). Occurrence of human remains with Pleistocene fossils, Lagow Sand Pit, Dallas, Texas. *Science,* 57(1472):333–334. Lancaster.
13. ———
14. Crook, Wilson W. (1961). A revised interpretation of the Lagow discovery, Texas. *Am. Antiq.* 26:545–547.
15. ———
16. Sellards, E.H. (1952). *Early Man in America: A Study in Prehistory.* Austin: University of Texas Press,
    Crook, W.W., Jr., and Harris, R.K. (1957). Hearths and artifacts of early man near Lewisville, Texas and associated faunal material. *Bull. Texas Archeol. Soc.* 28:7–97. Austin, Crook, Wilson W., Jr., and Harris, R.K. (1958). A Pleistocene Campsite near Lewisville, Texas. *Am. Antiq.* 23(3):233–246.
17. Museum at Southern Methodist University, Dallas, Texas.
18. ———

LAGUNA BEACH

1. Laguna Beach.
2. City of Laguna Beach, California, 33°32'N, 117°45'W.
3. Wilson, W.H., and Marriner, E.H. in 1933, during street grading.
4. Sediments in alluvial fan emanating from canyon at higher level in Laguna Mountains, California.
5. Not a burial.
6. Late Pleistocene. Late Wisconsin material redeposited in alluvial fan during Recent time.
7. Uncertain.
8. One of the human long bones contained fragments of *Mytilus californius* (mussel).
9. Human remains: cranium, F = 0.30%, N = 0.26%, eU308 = 60 ppm; long bone fragment F = 0.30% N = 0.23%, eU308 = 63 ppm.
10. A1: 17,150 ± 1,470 B.P. on bases of ^{14}C dating of residual collagen in human cranium (UCLA 1233A). Berger, R., and Libby, W.F. (1969) UCLA radiocarbon dates IX. *Radiocarbon* 11:194–195. Also: Postcranial fragments > 14,800 years B.P. (UCLA–1233 B) Berger, R. and Libby, W.F. (1969). UCLA Radiocarbon Dates IX, Radiocarbon II, 195.
11. Laguna 1. Adult cranium (f) and limb bones (ff). "Skull not dissimilar to recent Indian of Santa Barbara coast." T. Dale Stewart, *in* Berger and Libby (1969).
12. Laguna Beach newspaper, January 15, 1937.
13. Plhak, M. (1978). Die Morphologie der fossilen Hominiden von Los Angeles und Laguna Beach. *Zeits. f. Morphol. u. Anthropol.*, in press.
14. Berger, Rainer, Protsch, Reiner, Reynolds, Richard, Rozaire, Charles, and Sackett, James R. (1971). New radiocarbon dates based on bone collagen of California paleo-Indians. *Contrib. Univ. Calif. Archaeol. Res. Fac.* Berkeley, No. 12. Plhak, M. (1975). "Chronologie und Morphologie der frühesten Hominiden Amerikas." Masters Thesis, University of Frankfurt.
15. Riddel, F.A. (1969). Archaeology: Western Hemisphere Britannica Book of the year, pp. 100-104.
16. Berger, R., Horney, A.G. and Libby, W.F. (1964). Radiocarbon dating of bone and shell from their organic components. *Science* 144:999–1001.

17. W.H. Wilson, 22711 Vista del Sol, Laguna Beach, California.
18. Los Angeles County Museum, Los Angeles, California. J.W. Goethe Universität, 6000 Frankfurt a.M. Siesmayerstrasse 70, BRD, F. Weidenreich Institute of Anthropology, Dept. Palaeoanthropology and Archaeometry.

LINGER

1. Linger.
2. Linger blowout located in S section of San Luis Valley of south-central Colorado.
3. Middle 1960s, discoverer unknown. Rediscovered by J. Dowson in late 1960s.
4. *In situ* on surface of Linger blowout.
5. ——
6. ———
7. Surface find possibly of Folsom age.
8. ———
9. ———
10. ———
11. Partial calvarium, parts of frontal and both parietals. Parts of r. and l. superciliary arches, r. and l. supraorbital margins. Possibly female under 22 years of age. Dolichocranic nearly identical to Midland in overall skull measurements.
12. Patterson, D. and Agogino, G. (1976). The Linger skull. *Southwest Heritage* 6(2):22–25.
13. Patterson and Agogino, (1976).
14. ———
15. Patterson and Agogino (1976), pp. 22–25.
16. ———
17. Department of Anthropology, University of Toronto, Canada.
18. ———

LITTLE SYCAMORE

1. Little Sycamore.
2. Site Ven-1 is located in SW Ventura County, on a terraced seacliff promentory 1.2 miles W of the Los Angeles County Line, California.
3. Excavated by William James Wallace in 1952.
4. An open seacliff site, arealy 114 m by 151 m: from the surface, 5 cm unconsolidated black earth; 8 cm compacted, yellowish-red soil cemented by finely granular calcium carbonate; sterile base of reddish clay —— ideal section (Wallace 1954).
5. Fifteen burials: 5 flexed, 10 partial or secondary reburials.
6. Holocene.
7. Affinity with Oak Grove: 116 milling stones and 123 mullers, red ochre (Wallace 1954).
8. *Odocoileus hemionus* syn. *Cariacus macrotis* (Californian mule deer), *Enhydra lutris* (sea otter), *Phalacrocorax pygmaeus (P. aristotelis?)* (cormorant), *Podiceps griseigena (P. auritus/P. cristatus?)* (grebe), *Pelecanus sp.* (pelican), *Olivella* (probably *Olivia flammulata*), *Haiiotis rufescens* (red abalone), *Haliotis chacherodii* (black abalone), *Cypraea sp.* (cowry shell).
9. ——
10. ——
11. Little Sycamore 1–15. Thirteen adults, 2 children, plus "a vast quantity of dissociated and broken bones."
12. Wallace, William James (1954). The Little Sycamore site and the early milling stone cultures of Southern California. *Am. Antiq.* 20:112–123.
13. ——
14. ——
15. Wallace (1954), Figs. 41 and 42 of burials *in situ*.
16. Rogers, David Banks (1929). *Prehistoric Man of the Santa Barbara Coast*. Santa Barbara: Santa Barbara Museum of Natural History.
17. University of Southern California, Los Angeles, California.
18. ——

LOS ANGELES

1. Los Angeles.
2. Open site on the Los Angeles River near Los Angeles, California, 34°5'N, 118°15'W. Site No. LAn-172.
3. Discovered by workmen in 1936. Investigated by I.A. Lopatin, University of Southern California (1936).
4. Alluvium; bones from gravel 61-cm (2-ft) thick covered by clay and surface soil, a total thickness of 3.35 m (11 ft). Clements, T. (1938). Age of the "Los Angeles Man" deposits. *Am. J. Sci.,* Ser. 5, 36:137–141.

    Bowden, A.O., and Lopatin, I.a. (1936). Pleistocene man in southern California *Science* 84:507–508. New York.
5. ———
6. Late Pleistocene (Clements 1938).
7. ———
8. *Archidiscodon imperator* (extinct elephant) (Clements 1938).
9. Human calvaria: F = 0.04–0.12%, N = 0.02–0.03%, Associated fauna: *Archidiskodon* F = 0.08–0.15%, N = 0.04–0.05%. ". . . we must conclude that the fluorine determination indicates all of the bones are of approximately the same age." Heizer, R.F., and Cook, S.F. (1952). Fluorine and other chemical tests of some North American human and animal bones. *Am. J. Phys. Anthropol.* n.s., 10:289–304.
10. A1: 23,600 B.P. (UCLA-1430), collagen date from skull. A1 and R1: Ca. 28,000 B.P. Amino-acid (dating by J. Bada, info fide R. Berger, UCLA).
11. Los Angeles 1. "Los Angeles Man": adult, female: calvaria (f), "fragments of other bones."
12. Bowden and Lopatin (1936).
13. Lopatin, I.A. (1940). Fossil man in the vicinity of Los Angeles, California. *Proc. 6th Pacific Sci. Congr.* 4:177–181. Similar to "Basketmaker type." Plhak, M. (1978). Die Morphologie der fossilen Hominiden von Los Angeles and Laguna Beach. Zeits. f. Morphol. u. Anthropol., in press.
14. Berger, R., Protsch, Reiner, Reynolds, Rozaire, Charles, and Sackett, James (1971). New radiocarbon dates based on bone collagen of California paleo-Indians. *Contrib. Univ. Calif. Archaeol. Res. Fac.,* Berkeley, No. 12. Plhak, M. (1975).

"Chronologie und Morphologie der frühesten fossilen Hominiden Amerikas." Masters Thesis, University of Frankfurt.

15. Lopatin (1940).
16. Clements (1938). Heizer, R.F. (1950). Observations on early man in California. University of California Archaeological Survey Reports, No. 7, pp. 5-9. Berkeley. Heizer, R.F. (1952). A Review of Problems in the Antiquity of Man in California. University of California Archaeological Survey Reports, No. 16, pp. 3-17. Berkeley. Hrdlicka (1937). Early Man in America: What have the bones to say? In Early Man, pp. 93-104, Philadelphia: J.B. Lippincott Co.
17. Los Angeles County Museum, Los Angeles, California.
18. J.W. Goethe Universität, F. Weidenreich Institute of Anthropology, Dept. Paleoanthropology and Archeometry, 6 Frankfurt a.M., Siesmayerstr. 70, BRD.

MARMES

1. Marmes.
2. Open site on buried flood plain (now flooded by reservoir) immediately in front of Marmes Rockshelter, near W bank of the Palouse River 2.4 km ($1\frac{1}{2}$ miles) N of its confluence with the Snake River, Franklin County, SE Washington. 46°37'N, 118°12'W.
3. R. Fryxell, Department of Anthropology, Washington State University, Pullman, and R.J. Marmes, owner of the Marmes ranch, in July 1965.
4. Scattered on and in lacustrine sediment forming buried surface of an abandoned floodplain of the Palouse River. Fryxell, R., Bielicki, T., Daugherty, R.D., Gustafson, C., Irwin, H.T., and Keel, B.C. (1968), Human remains of mid- Pinedale age from southeastern Washington, *Am. Antiq.* 33:511–515.
5. ———
6. Mid-Pinedale Stage of the Rocky Mountains, and related quaternary history of the Columbia Plateau, *in* Wright, H.E., Jr. and Frey, D.G. eds. (1965), *The Quaternary of the United States,* Princeton: Princeton University Press, pp. 231–242.
7. A cylindrical bone needle, flattened on one side (R. Fryxell *et al.* 1968).
8. *Cervus elaphus* (deer), *Cervus canadensis* (canadian deer), *Antilocapra americana* (American antelope), unidentified micromammalia, Pisces, Mollusca (R. Fryxell *et al.* 1968).
9. ———
10. A2/A3: ca. 11,000 B.P. on basis of radiocarbon dating of river mussel shells from sediment overlying the hominid material: 10,750 ± 100 B.P. (WSU-211), 10,810 ± 275 B.P. (WSU-363), 10,475 ± 270 B.P. (WSU-366) (R. Fryxell *et al.* 1968). The hominid material was deposited in a lake that filled the canyon of the Palouse and Snake Rivers after the eruption of the Glacier Peak, marked by volcanic ash in the lake sediments. The Glacier Peak eruption is dated 12,000 ± 310 B.P. (WSU-155). Fryxell, R. (1965), Mazama and Glacier Peak volcanic ash layers: relative ages, *Science* 147:1288–1290. New York.
11. Marmes 1. "Marmes Man." Young adult: lt. parietale (ff), rt. parietale (f), occipitale (f), frontale (f), cranial fragments, rt. ramus mandibulae (f), 1M (ff), costae, vertebrae, postcranial fragments (R. Fryxell *et al.* 1968).
12. R. Fryxell *et al.* (1968).

13. R. Fryxell *et al.* (1968). *Homo sapiens,* with some Mongoloid features (R. Fryxell *et al.* 1968).

14. ————

15. R. Fryxell *et al.* (1968), p. 513.

16. Fryxell, R. (1963). Through a mirror darkly: a geologist's interpretation of man's changing environment. *The Record,* Washington State University Library 1-18.
     Fryxell, R., and Daugherty, R.D. (1962). Interim Report: archaeological salvage in the Lower Monumental Reservoir, *Rep. Invest. Lab. Anthrop. Wash. St. University,* Pullman, Washington, No. 21.
     Fryxell, R. and Daugherty, R.D. (1965). Fig. 41 (correlation chart) in *Guidebook for Field Conference F. Northern and Middle Rocky Mountains (8th Conf. Int. Assoc. Quatern. Res.),* Lincoln, p. 84., eds. Fryxell, R. and Daugherty, R.D.
     Riddell, F.A. (1969). Archaeology: western hemisphere. *Britannica Book of the Year:* 100–104.

17. Laboratory of Anthropology, Washington State University, Pullman, Washington.

18. ————

McKEAN

1. McKean.
2. South side of the Belle Fourche River $3\frac{1}{4}$ miles above Keyhole Dam, $\frac{3}{4}$ of a mile to the SE of the river channel, Crook County, NE Wyoming (48-Ck-7).
3. ———
4. Open terrace, stained sand and charcoal lenses, depth 1.1–4.2 ft.
5. More likely a "skull cache."
6. Holocene (ca. 5,000 B.P.).
7. McKean. "Similar to but not equal to Signal Butte I" (i.e., Archaic) (Mulloy 1954).
8. Fauna in direct association with McKean calvaria but probably not contemporary: *Bison* sp., 2 ossa innominates (f).
9. ———
10. ———
11. McKean 1. Female calvaria of Neumann's "Deneid" variety.
12. Mulloy, William B., (1954). The McKean site. *Southwestern J. Anthropol.* 10(4):432–460. Albuquerque.
13. Stewart, T. Dale (1954). The lower level human skull. Appendix *in* Mulloy (1954), pp. 457–59.
14. ———
15. Stewart (1954), p. 458.
16. ———
17. United States National Museum, Washington, D.C. University of Wyoming.
18. ———

MEDICINE CROW

1. Medicine Crow Site (39 BF 2).
2. Buffalo County, South Dakota, left and E bank of Missouri River. Five miles NW of Fort Thompson across the river from Lower Brule.
3. W.N. Irving in September 1957.
4. Relative depth RD 65; in silt deposit. No exact depth by metric measurements given.
5. Probably displacement from former burial. Skull was found without postcranial remains. One individual.
6. Undetermined (Early Holocene?) ca. 7,000–4,000 B.P.
7. Below Duncan point horizon. General association with Fluted point, a Plainview point.
8. Association, but not specifically mentioned by name.
9. Measurements of adsorbed alpha and beta radiation. No specific technique given, no percentages of measurements.
10. ———
11. Complete cranium. Young adult male. Mesocranic, orthocranial, and mesocephalic. Similar to Brown's Valley Man. Indianoid.
12. Stephenson, R.L. (1958). Notes and News. *Am. Antiq.* 23:335–338.
    Stephenson, R.L. (1959). Notes and News. *Am. Antiq.* 24:337–340.
13. Bass, W.M. (1976). An early Indian cranium from the Medicine Crow site, (39 BF2), Buffalo County, South Dakota." *Am. J. Phys. Anthrop.,* 45:695–700.
14. ———
15. Bass (1976). p. 697.
16. Coogan, A., and Irving, W. (1959). Late Pleistocene and Recent missouri River terraces in the Big Bend Reservoir, South Dakota. *Proc. Iowa Acad. Sci.* 66:317–327.
17. ———
18. ———

MELBOURNE

1. Melbourne.
2. Open site near the town of Melbourne, Brevard County, Florida; 3.2 km (2 miles) W of Indian River, 2.4 km (1.5 miles) W of railroad station, 91.4 m (100 yd) S of Route 192; 28°10′N, 80°45′W.
3. F.B. Loomis, J.W. Gidley, and C.P. Singleton, June 26, 1925.
4. Fifteen centimeters (6 in.) deep in layer 2 of the Melbourne Formation. Gidley, J.W., and Loomis, F.B. (1926). Fossil man in Florida. *Am. J. Sci.*, Ser. 5, 12:254–264.
5. Human bones and artifacts probably intrusive from overlying contact with Van Valkenburg Formation. Rouse, I. (1951). A survey of Indian River archaeology, Florida. *Yale Univ. Publ. Anthropol.* 44:153–165.
6. Early Holocene.
7. Five stone and bone artifacts, including a projectile point and bone pin, probably preceramic cultural period (Rouse 1951).
8. *Megalonyx jeffersoni* (giant ground sloth), *Mammonteus americanus (M. primigenius?)* (mammoth), *Equus occidentalis* (extinct horse). Gazin, C.L. (1950). Annotated list of fossil Mammalia associated with human remains at Melbourne, Florida. *J. Washington Acad. Sci.* 40:397–404.
9. Melbourne 1 tibia: F = 0.096%, N = 0.052%; "Associated" fauna: *Equus*, F = 0.119%, N = 0.075%; *Mammuthus*, F = 0.116%, N = 0.047%.
   "contemporaneity of human bones and fauna not demonstrated with certainty." Heizer, R.F., and Cook, S.F. (1952). Fluorine and other chemical tests of some North American human and animal bones. *Am. J. Phys. Anthropol.*, n.s., 10:289–303.
10. ⸻
11. Melbourne 1. "Melbourne Man" adult female: cranium (f), mandibula (f), lt. clavicula (f), 2 humeri (ff), lt. ulna (ff), 1 metacarpal (f), 2 tibiae (ff), lt. fibula (ff), unidentified skeletal fragments.
12. Gidley and Loomis (1926).
13. Stewart, T.D. (1946). A re-examination of the fossil human skeletal remains from Melbourne, Florida, with further data on the Vero skull. *Smithsonian Misc. Coll.* 106 (10):1–28.

14. Not typical of recent Florida Indians. (Stewart 1946). Plhak, M. (1975). "Chronologie und Morphologie der frühesten fossilen Hominiden Amerikas." Masters Thesis, University of Frankfurt.
15. Stewart (1946).
16. Hrdlicka, Ales (1937). Early man in America: What have the bones to say? *in* MacGurdy, G.G. (ed.) (1937). *Early Man.* Philadelphia: J.B. Lippincott Co.: 95–98.
    Rouse, I. (1950). Vero and Melbourne Man: A cultural and chronological interpretation. *Trans. N.Y. Acad. Sci.,* Ser. 2, 12:220–224.
17. United States National Museum, Physical Anthropology Division, Washington, D.C. Cat. No. 331402.
18. ———

MIDLAND

1. Midland.
2. Surface site, wind deflated, near Midland, Texas. 31°55′N, 102°07′W.
3. K. Glasscock in 1953. Investigated by F. Wendorf, Museum of New Mexico in 1954.
4. Grey sand unit, Judkins Formation. Wendorf, F., Krieger, A.D., Albritton, C., and Stewart, T.D. (1955), The Midland Discovery: A report on the Pleistocene Human Remains from Midland, Texas. Austin: University of Texas Press.
5. Burial, believed to be contemporaneous with occupation of grey sand unit.
6. Terminal Late Pleistocene: Scharbaur Interval. Wendorf, F. (ed.) (1961). *Palaeoecology of the Llano Estacado*, 121–133.
   Wendorf *et al.* (1955).
7. Paleo-Indian, Midland Complex. Wendorf, F., and Krieger, A.D. (1959), New Light on the Midland discovery. *Am. Antiq.* 25:66–78.
8. *Equus occidentalis* (extinct horse), *Capromeryx sp.* (extinct pronghorn antelope), *Bison antiquus figginsi* (bison) (F. Wendorf *et al.* 1955).
9. Midland 1. Calvaria: $F = 0.71–0.86\%$, $N = 0.031–0.325\%$, $eU308 = 13.15 \pm 1.74$ ppm (average).
   Midland 1. Costa: $F = $ calvaria: $F = 0.59\%$.
   Associated fauna: *Equus* tooth: $F = 0.96\%$, $eU308 = 29.37 \pm 1.93$ ppm, $N = 0.01\%$. *Equus* radius: $F = 0.98\%$, $eU308 = 10.83 \pm 1.74$ ppm, $N = 0.20\%$.
   Modern fauna from overlying unit including *Lepus*: $F = 0.019–0.025\%$, $N = 2.465–2.416\%$, $eU\ 308 = < 1.00$ ppm.
   Wendorf *et al.* (1955).
   Oakley, K.P. and Rixon, A.E. (1958), Radioactivity of materials from the Scharbauer site, near Midland Texas, *Am. Antiq.* 24:185–187.
10. A2: $7,100 \pm 1,000$ B.P. (M-411) on basis of ^{14}C dating of fossil bone from grey sand unit. A2/A3: 14,700 B.P. on basis of ^{14}C dating of terrestrial gastropod shell from underlying white sand unit: $13,400 \pm 1300$ B.P. (L-304C). Probably $< 9,270$ B.P. on basis of ^{14}C dating fossil bone and mammoth tusk from underlying white sand unit: $8,670 \pm 600$ B.P. (M-389-391 combined). For discussion of dating see Wendorf and Krieger (1959) pp. 75–78.

11. Midland 1. "Midland Man," young adult female, 25–30 years: calvaria (f), phalanges manus (f), clavicula (ff), skeletal fragments.
12. Wendorf *et al.* (1955).
13. Wendorf *et al.* (1955).
14. Plhak, M. (1975). "Chronologie und Morphologie der frühesten Hominiden Amerikas." Masters Thesis, University of Frankfurt.
15. Wendorf *et al.* (1955).
16. ———
17. Museum of New Mexico, Santa Fe, New Mexico.
18. University Museum, University of Pennsylvania, Philadelphia, Pennsylvania.

MINNESOTA

1. Minnesota.
2. Open site, near Pelican Rapids, Otter Trail County, 32 km (20 miles) N of Fergus Falls, Minnesota. 46°35'N, 96°07'W.
3. P.F. Stary, June 18, 1931. Investigated by A.E. Jenks, University of Minnesota (1932-1934).
4. In a varved silt, such as those found in Lake Aggassiz, 4–5 m (10–12 ft) below surface of a hill stripped by road cutting activities. Jenks, A.E. (1936). Pleistocene man in Minnesota: A fossil *Homo sapiens*. Minneapolis:

   Antevs, E. (1937). The age of "Minnesota Man" *Yearbook Carnegie Inst. Washington* 36:335–338.

   Bryan, K., and MacClintock, P. (1938). What is implied by "disturbance" at the site of Minnesota Man. *J. Geol.* 46:279–292.
5. Probably a burial. *CHF:* 298.
6. Holocene.
7. No specific culture; associated artifacts include an antler dagger and a conch shell pendant. Probably Early Archaic (Jenks 1936).
8. Rodentia, including *Cavia* (guinea pigs); Reptilia (Jenks 1936).
9. ———
10. ———
11. Minnesota 1. "Minnesota Man." Female, about 15 years: almost complete skeleton, including cranium and mandibula (f).
12. Jenks (1936).
13. Hrdlicka, A. (1937). The Minnesota "Man" *Am. J. Phys. Anthropol.* 22:175–199. Sioux Indian type.
14. ———
15. Jenks (1936).
16. Jenks, A.E. (1938). A reply to a review by Dr. A. Hrdlicka. *Am. Anthropol.* 30:328–336.
17. Department of Anthropology, University of Minnesota, Minneapolis, Minnesota. Cat. No. 34.
18. ———

MULBERRY CREEK

1. Mulberry Creek.
2. Lauderdale Focus-type site CT°27 was located on the left bank of Mulberry Creek at its junction with the Tennessee River, in Sec. 22, Twp. 2S, Range 13W, Colbert County, Alabama.
3. Excavated by J.R. Foster, supervisor, in 1936–1938.
4. Stratified open midden of burned sand, flint, dense shell, water-borne sand, and earth, laid down on a sterile sloping sand bar. Arealy the site measured 5.08 m by 7.62 m and achieved a maximum depth of 46 cm.
5. Four types of burials: type 1 (oldest), round grave; type 2, flexed; type 3, extended; type 4, cremations.
6. Holocene; estimated less than 5,000 B.P.
7. Early Lauderdale Focus (below 30-cm depth worked flint was found to be negligible and was therefore termed the "worked bone zone"): bone projectile points, splitbone awls, 1 fish hook of 36 cm, 1 pestle, 1 lapstone, 1 stone cylinder.
8. Common freshwater mussels.
9. ————
10. ————
11. Mulberry Creek 1–134. Burials below 30 cm as follows: Type 1, round grave, flexed, on left side:
    MC 19. (30 cm).
    MC 74. (32 cm).
    MC 84. (33 cm).
    MC 89. (35 cm).
    MC 92. (30 cm): male.
    MC 93. (30 cm).
    Type 3, extended, or slightly flexed:
    83. (35 cm): 3 flint projectile points in ribs. Male, young adult.
    84. (35 cm): Male, mature adult: 4 flint projectile points in thorax, 2 in spine, 1 in mouth; missing hands, ulnae, radii.
    85. (35 cm): Male, adolescent: "cache" with burial containing 2 bone awls, 2 flints points, 1 flint knife; another flint point of a type foreign to the mound series was found in the spine; "leg bones missing."

86. (35 cm): stone cylinder.

88. (28 cm): Male: associated were 11 flint points, bone tools, 2 dogs.

Type 4, cremations:

79. (32 cm).

12. Webb, William S., and DeJarnette, Davis L., (1942). An archaeological survey of Pickwick Basin in the adjacent portions of the states of Alabama, Mississippi, and Tennessee. *Bulletin of the Bureau of American Ethnology,* No. 129. Washington, D.C.

13. Newman, Marshall T., and Snow, Charles E. Au (1942) *In* Webb, W.S., and DeJarnette, D.L. (1942). Preliminary report on the skeletal material from Pickwick Basin, Alabama. pp. 397–507. Pages 431–433: The Ct°27 submound Skeletons, treats burials, 83, 84, 85, 88,* and 92. ''The submound skeletons represent a more rugged variant of the Shell-Mound population.'' Undeformed dolichocranic type.

14. ——

15. Webb and DeJarnette (1942), plates 274, 275, 281, 289, 290, 300, and 302, views of five burials *in situ*.

16. ——

17. University of Kentucky.

18. ——

(*A 28 cm burial).

NATCHEZ

1. Natchez.
2. Open site, 9.6 km (6 miles) E of Natchez, Mississippi. 31=40'N, 91°15'W.
3. M.W. Dickson in 1846.
4. Blue clay beneath "diluvial" drift. Anon. (1846). *Proc. Acad. nat. Sci.* 3:106–107.
5. ———
6. Late Pleistocene?
7. ———
8. Hominid bone found 60 cm (2 ft) below 3 associated skeletons of *Megalonyx jeffersoni* (giant ground sloth). Other fauna included *"Ereptodon"* (solitary edentate tooth), *Mylodon sp.* (giant ground sloth). *Mastodon americanus* (mastodon), *Equus occidentalis* (extinct horse), and *Bison antiquus figginsi* (bison) (large horned). Anon. (1846).
   Schmidt, E. (1872). Zur Urgeschichte Nordamerikas. *Archiv Anthropol.* 5:244–250.
   Wilson, T. (1895). On the presence of fluorine as a test for the fossilization of animals bones. *Am. Naturalist* 29:301–317, 434–456, 719–725.
9. Natchez 1 os coxae: F = 0.38%. Associated *Mylodon*: F = 0.28%. T. Wilson (1895, p. 722).
   Stewart, T.D. (1951). The Antiquity of Man in America Demonstrated by the Fluorine Test, *Science* 113:391–392, New York. New analyses for CFH: Natchez 1: F = 0.88%, 100F/P205 = 3.4, N = 1.42%. *Mylodon halani* bone: F = 0.99%, 100F/P205 = 4.9, N = 1.59%.
10. ———
11. Natchez 1. "Natchez Pelvis." Adult male: rt. os coxae (f).
12. Anon. (1846).
13. E. Schmidt (1872).
14. ———
15. ———
16. Lyell, C. (1863). *The Antiquity of Man,* London: Au: Publ. pp. 200205. Richards, W.A. (1951). Vindication of Natchez Man. *Frontiers* 15:139–140.
    Quimby, G.I., (1956). The locus of the Natchez pelvis find. *Am. Antiq.* 22:77–78.

Wormington, H.M. (1957). *Ancient Man in North America*. Denver Mus. Nat. Hist. (2nd ed., Popular Science, No. 4) p. 226. Leidy, T. (1889). Notice of some fossil human bones. *Wagner Free Inst. Sci. Trans.* 2:9–12.

17. The Academy of Natural Sciences of Philadelphia, Philadelphia, Pennsylvania. Cat. No. 12452.

18. ————

NEBRASKA "LOESS MAN" (GILDER MOUND)

1. Nebraska (Gilder Mound).
2. On "Longs' Hill" situated near and running parallel with the Missouri, about 4.8 km N of Florence and 16 km N of Omaha, Nebraska.
3. F.T. Parker, William Morris, and Charles S. Huntington, in June 1894; R.F. Gilder in 1906.
4. Open, artificial mound: 76 cm disturbed top soil; 61 cm calcined clay, shell, and quartzite spalls, or "loess"; 10 cm of hardened, compact earth (original top of the loess hill).
5. Older remains, 11–30 cm, disarticulated.
6. ". . . the loess here is not leached of lime salts . . . arguing for recency of deposition, ... rests on Kansan drift, and though as young as the later Wisconsin sheet or younger, it is nevertheless old" (Barbour, 1907).
7. None at lower levels.
8. ———
9. ———
10. ———
11. Nebraska 1. (91 cm) male, past middle age; incomplete calvaria (nearly dolichocephalic)
    2. (91 cm) female (?) adult: "very defective" skull.
    3. (1.22 m) female adult: frontal and parietals bearing "surface marks of cutting."
    4. (1.83 m) male adult: frontal and parietals bearing "surface marks of cutting."
    5. Abnormal frontal only.
    6. (1.52 m) male adult: calvaria (mesocephalic); upper face and lower jaw found near specimen cannot be fitted because of defects in reconstruction.
    7. (Not described in Hrdlicka 1907)
    8. (1.52 m) male adult: calvaria (mesocephalic); "neanderthaloid" in deficient vaulting of forehead.
    9. (Not described in Hrdlicka 1907).
    10. (Shallow) subadult: cranium (brachycephalic); part of occipital cut away.

11. (1.22 m) male adult: frontal only.
12. (1.22 m) "young": mandible with 3 molars.
13. ("Deep") male: mandible, left horizontal ramus.
14. (1.52 m) female: left vertical ramus of mandible.
15. Humeri: 5 entire and 12 (f).
16. ("Deep") humerus: shaft planoconvex; lacking lower end.
17. ("Deep") female adult: ulna with cuts.
18. Radii: 3 entire.
19. Femora: 8 entire and 9 (f), and 3 subadult.
20. Tibiae: 2 entire and 10 (f).
21. Fibula: 1 adult.
22. (1.52 m) scapula with cut edge.
23. ("Deep") ribs: 3 (f), 1 with cuts.
24. ("Deep") "several dorsal and lumbar vertebrae."
25. ("Deep") sacrum.
26. Male adult: 2 pelves.
27. ("Deep") os calcis.
28. ("Deep") "several phalanges and pieces thereof."
29. ("Deep") child, less than 1 year: long bones.

12. Barbour, E.H., and Ward, H.B. (1906). Discovery of an early type of man in Nebraska. *Science,* Nov. 16.
13. Hrdlicka, Ales (1907). *Skeletal Remains Suggesting or Attributed to Early Man in North America.* Bulletin 33. Washington, D.C. Bureau of American Ethnology.
14. ———
15. Hrdlicka (1907).
16. Hrdlicka (1907), bibliography p. 70.
17. University of Nebraska, Lincoln, Nebraska.
18.———

RENIER

1. Renier.
2. Fossil beach of Green Bay (Lake Algonquin). Lake Michigan; site owned by Paul Renier, SE quarter of the NE quarter of Sec. 29, Twp. 25N, Range 22E, Town of Scott, Brown County, Wisconsin (New Franken Quadrangle).
3. Ronald J. Mason and Carol Irwin in 1959; excavation by Mason and Irwin in 1959.
4. Aeolean sand above beach deposits. Thwaites, F.T., and Bertrand, Kenneth (1957). Pleistocene geology of the Door Peninsula, Wisconsin. *Bull. Geol. Soc. Am.* 68:831–880. Washington, D.C.
5. Cremation burial.
6. Holocene; post-Algonquin. "An age of 6,500 to 4,000 B.C. is suggested for the burial" (Mason and Irwin 1960).
7. Eden-Scottsbluff; Early Archaic.
8. ———
9. ———
10. A3: 6,300 ± 150 B.P. for other Eden-Scottsbluff points (Wormington, 1957); other Scottsbluff points, 6,876 ± 250 B.P., 9,524 ± 450 B.P. (Libby 1955).
11. Renier 1. Adolescent: mandible (ff), palatine (ff); calcined bones of postcranial skeleton not identifiable.
12. Mason, J. and Irwin, C. (1960). An Eden-Scottsbluff burial in northeastern Wisconsin. *Am. Antiq.* 26:43–57.
13. Charles E. Lyman, *in* Mason and Irwin (1960), *Am. Antiquity* 26:45.
14. ———
15. ———
16. ———
17. Neville Public Museum, 129 Jefferson Street, Green Bay, Wisconsin.
18. ———

ROCK BLUFF

1. Rock Bluff.
2. ". . . at Rock Bluff, on the Illinois River where it crossed the fortieth parallel" (Meigs 1868), Illinois.
3. By "McConnel" in 1866; sent to Joseph Henry, of the Smithsonian Institution, in 1866.
4. ". . . in a fissure . . . . filled with the drift material of this region, consisting of clay, sand, and broken stone, the whole being covered with a stratum of surface soil . . . . which apparently had been undisturbed since the deposit . . . at a depth of three feet" (Meigs 1868).
5. ———
6. ". . . the Champlain, or even to the glacial, epoch." (Schmidt 1871–1872).
7. ———
8. ———
9. ———
10. ———
11. Rock Bluff 1. Male: cranium (dolichocephalic), "remarkably well preserved."
    2. Mandible (apparently of another person).
12. Meigs, J. Aitken (1868). Description of a human skull in the collection of the Smithsonian Institution. *Smithsonian Report for 1867*. Washington, D.C.: Smithsonian Institution, pp. 412–415.
13. Meigs (1868).
14. ———
15. Hrdlicka (1907) (one lateral view).
16. Schmidt, E. (1871–1872.). Zur Urgeschichte Nordamerikas. *Archiv Anthropol.*, 5:237–244. Braunschweig: Vieweg Verlag.
    Kollman, J. (1884). Hohes Alter der Menschenrassen. *Z. Ethnol.* XVI: 191–193. Braunschweig: Vieweg Verlag.
    Hrdlicka, Ales (1907). *Skeletal Remains Suggesting or Attributed to Early Man in North America*. Bulletin *33,* Washington, D.C.: Bureau of American Ethnology.
17. United States National Museum, Washington D.C. Cat. No. 243881.
18. ———

RIVERVIEW CEMETARY

1. Riverview Cemetary.
2. Riverview Cemetary near Trenton, New Jersey.
3. In 1887 by a grave digger who gave it to a Mr. Volk who presented it to the Peabody Museum.
4. In an elevated part of the ground with a few black lines in the soil at a depth of about 91 cm, in apparently undisturbed, stratified sand and gravel (paraphrased from Hrdlicka's (1907) excerpt of the *Bulletin*).
5. ———
6. Unknown (probably Recent).
7. ———
8. ———
9. ———
10. ———
11. Riverview Cemetary 1. Male, middle aged: calvaria (chamoecephalic).
12. Anon. (1902). *Bull. Am. Mus. Nat. Hist.* XVI:
13. Anon. (?) (1902).
14. Hrdlicka, Ales (1907). *Skeletal Remains Suggesting or Attributed to Early Man in North America*. Bulletin 33. Washington, D.C.: Bureau of American Ethnology. Similar to chamoecephalic skulls of Bremen, Germany; not Indian.
15. Hrdlicka (1907).
16. ———
17. Peabody Museum, Harvard University, Cambridge, Massachusetts. Cat. No. 44280.
18. ———

SAUK VALLEY

1. Sauk Valley.
2. Gravel pit on the Land of Daniel W. Frazer; Lot 1 of the NE quarter, Sec. 11, Twp. 127N, Range 35W, in West Union Township, Todd County, Minnesota.
3. Workman Earl Tompkins in June 1935; investigated by A.E. Jenks (1936). Pleistocene Man in Minnesota: A fossil *Homo Sapiens*. The University of Minnesota Press, Minneapolis, Minnesota.
4. Undisturbed gravel bed—the West Union Gravel—within late Wisconsin moraine of the Altamont-Gary series; not, however, firmly established (Bryan *et al.* 1938).
5. Probably entombed by natural process; the brain case was filled at the time of discovery with packed limonitic sand of the same quality of the gravels in which it was interred.
6. Terminal Pleistocene, "Sauk Valley Man is of considerable antiquity, probably even earlier than Browns Valley Man, for whom a date of 8,000 to 12,000 years ago is assigned" (Jenks and Wilford 1938).
7. ———
8. ———
9. ———
10. ———
11. Sauk Valley 1. "Sauk Valley Man." Male, middle-aged adult: cranium, mandible; of the post cranial skeleton the following bones were recovered: 2 clavicles (f), 2 thoracic and 1 lumbar vertebrae, 14 ribs (f), 2 innominates (f), 2 humeri, 2 radii (f) 2 ulnae (f), 2 femora, 2 tibiae rt. comp., lt. (f), rt. fibula (f), rt. astragalus, and rt. 1st metatarsal.
12. Bryan, Kirk, Retzek, Henry, and McCann, Franklin T. (1938). Discovery of Sauk Valley Man of Minnesota, with an account of the geology. *Bull. Texas Archaeol. Paleontol. Soc.* 10:114–135. Abilene.
13. Jenks, Albert E., and Wilford, Lloyd A. (1938). The Sauk Valley skeleton. *Bull. Texas Archaeol. Paleontol. Soc.* 10:136–169. Abilene. (Compares with Minnesota and Browns Valley men.)
14. ———

15. Jenks and Wilford (1938).
16. ———
17. Department of Anthropology, University of Minnesota, Minnesota.
18. ———

SCRIPPS ESTATES (LA JOLLA) (SAN DIEGO MAN)

1. Scripps Estates (La Jolla).
2. University of California Archaeological Survey site SDi-525; San Diego Museum of Man site SDM-W9; Smithsonian Institution site SDC-535. The site lies along the seaward edge of the mesa complex that further inland is called Kearney Mesa and Linda Vista Mesa in W San Diego County, California, at 32°52′16–23″N, 117°14′53–56″W.
3. Earliest archaeologic work done by Malcolm J. Rodgers in the 1930s; extensive excavation by Shumway, Hubbs and Moriarty in 1958–1959.
4. Open mesa site on seacliff terrace fill, with the average elevation above sea level generally 110–120 m. The terrace fill encompasses the entire Wisconsin Epoch (Hubbs). The shell midden averages a depth of less than 1 m in the area of concentrated burials (Shumway, *et al.* 1961).
5. Forty-six burials excavated.
6. Holocene.
7. La Jolla culture.
8. Fifty-six species of pelecypod and gastropod mollusks; misc. Pisces.
9. ———
10. A1: Aspartic acid on hominid bones, ca. 40,000 B.P. possibly off by at least 5,000 years or more (see appendix after item 18).

    A2: Four ^{14}C dates based on treatment of *Mytilus californianus,* acetylene method: (LJ-79): 6,700 ± 150 B.P. (associated with burial 7); (LJ-109): 7,370 ± 100 B.P. (B₁ horizon, lowest occupied); (LJ-110): 5,460 ± 100 B.P. (A horizon, latest occupied); (LJ-221): 5,740 ± 140 B.P. (B₁ horizon) (Hubbs *et al.,* 1960).
11. Scripps Estates 1–46. Two examples (see appendix after item 18):

    S.E. 3. Adult male: nearly complete and in good condition except for small bones of hands and feet; long bones articulated, including patella. Preserved *in situ* at the site location.

    S.E. 10. Adult female (?): nearly complete and in fair condition (exacavated, described by Warren in Moriarty *et al.* 1959).
12. Moriarty, J.R., Shumway, G., and Warren, C.N. (1959). Scripps Estates site I (Sdi-525) A preliminary report on an early site on the San Diego coast.

Archaeological Survey Annual Report 1958–1959. Los Angeles: Department of Anthropology and Sociology, UCLA pp. 185–216.

13. Warren *in* Moriarty *et al.* (1959).
14. Shumway, G., Hubbs, C.L., and Moriarty, J.R., (1961). Scripps Estate site, San Diego, California: A La Jolla site dated 5,460 to 7,370 years before the present. *N. Y. Acad. Sci. Ann.* 93:37–132. New York.
15. ———
16. Hubbs, C.L., Bien, G.S., and Suess, H.E. (1960). La Jolla natural radiocarbon measurements I. *Am. J. Sci. Radiocarbon Suppl.* 2:197–223.
17. Several preserved *in situ;* others at San Diego Museum of Man, San Diego Museum of Natural History, University of California, Los Angeles.
18. ———

Appendix (see item 11).

A series of relative dates (absolute ?) were obtained from osteologic material from the above sites: Bada, J.L., Schroeder, R.A., and Carter, G.F. (1974). New Evidence for the Antiquity of Man in North America Deduced from Aspartic Acid Racemization. *Science* 184:791–793.

The dates are as follows:

SDM 18402   6,000
SDM 16755   28,000
SDM 16742   44,000
SDM 16704   48,000

At the meetings of the SWAA Congress, San Diego, California, in April 1977, Bada reported again on these dates and others over 50,000 years B.P. In the light of inaccuracies of amino acid dating, which at the present state of research are numerous, these dates should be viewed with utmost scepticism, especially as well-controlled radiocarbon dates exist for these same sites dating them to a maximum of 7,370 years B.P. (see under item 10).

STANFORD

1. Stanford 2.
2. Open site opposite the site of the Stanford residence in Palo Alto, California. 37°30'N, 112°15'W.
3. B. Seymour, in April–May 1922.
4. Gravels.
5. ———
6. Early Holocene. Heizer, R.F. (p. 150). T.D. McCowan (1950). The Stanford skull, a probable early man from Santa Clara County, California. *Rept. Univ. Calif. Archaeol. Surv.* No. 6:1-9, Berkeley.
7. ———
8. ———
9. Stanford 2: F = 0.27%, N = 1.24%.
10. A1: 4,530 ± 125 (UCLA-1425A) on basis of ^{14}C in collagen of calvarial bone, A1: 4,400 ± 120 (UCLA-1425B) on basis of ^{14}C in burnt bone. Berger, R., and Libby, W.F., UCLA *Radiocarbon* Dates 12: in preparation.
11. Stanford 2. "Stanford Man," adult male: calvaria (f).
12. Willis, B. (1922). Out of the long past. *The Stanford Cardinal, October 8–11* 1922.
13. Heizer (1950). McCown, T.D. (1950). The Stanford skull: The physical characteristics. University of California Archaeological Survey Reports, No. 6, pp. 10-17. Berkeley. Aboriginal type of California Indian.
14. ———
15. Heizer (1950).
16. Wormington, H.M. (1957). *Ancient Man in North America.* (4th edn.) Denver (Denver Mus. Nat. Hist. "Pop. Ser.," No. 4): p. 230.
17. Stanford Geological Museum, Stanford University, Palo Alto, California. Cat. No. 2915.
18. ———

TECOLOTE POINT

1. Tecolote Point.
2. Open seacliff promentory on the NW coast of Santa Rosa Island, at Tecolote Point, 49.81 km SW of Santa Barbara, California.
3. 1947; Phil C. Orr.
4. An upper layer of white, aeolean sand; up to 10 cm of black shell midden; 25–51 cm of white aeolean beach sand dune.
5. Seventy-nine burials, ⅓ buried in unique sitting position (for California), many with heads colored red but with a dye other than red ochre (hematite) — "red heads."
6. Holocene.
7. Three hundred thirty-four shell, 19 bone, 11 ground stone, 8 chipped stone, 2 asphalt mold (basket) artifacts. "Dune Dweller."
8. *Haliotis rufescens* (red abalone), *Haliotis chacherodii* (black abalone), *Olivella (Olivia flammulata), Trivia californiana* (mollusks) *Trivela stultorum* (mollusks).
9. ———
10. A1: 3,970 ± 100 B.P. (UCLA-140) on basis of residual collagen from "other human bones from a Santa Rosa Island canalino" (Berger *et al.* 1964).
    A2: On basis of samples of the abalone feature on the north edge of cemetary A *(Haliotis rufescens)*: 7,070 ± 300 B.P. (L-290D); 7,120 ± 400 B.P. (UCLA-663A); outer carbonate; 7,210 ± 400 B.P. (UCLA-663C), organic material; 7,230 ± 120 B.P. (UCLA-663B), inner carbonate.
11. Tecolote Point 1–79. One subadult, 4 young, 34 adult, 23 "gummers," 17 undetermined (upper mesocranic).
12. Orr, Phil C. (1952). Review of Santa Barbara Channel Archaeology. *Southwest J. Anthropol. 8(2):211–226.*
13. ———
14. Orr, Phil. C. (1968). *Prehistory of Santa Rosa Island.* Santa Barbara: Santa Barbara Museum of Natural History.
15. Orr (1968), plates 35–38, burials *in situ.*
16. Rogers, D.B. (1929). *Prehistoric Man of the Santa Barbara Coast.* Sant Barbara: Santa Barbara Museum of Natural History.

Meighan, C.W. (1959). California cultures and the concept of the archaic stage. *Am. Antiq.* 24:289–305.

17. Santa Barbara Museum of Natural History, Santa Barbara, California.
18. ———

TORRINGTON

1. Torrington.
2. Open face of a dynamited roadway cliff, near the N bank of the North Platte River, Wyoming, in the face of a low bluff.
3. Road gang, in 1935; investigated by W.W. Howells (1936?).
4. In a cave of crevice filled by rainwash; cave or crevice of Miocene sandstone (Howells 1938).
5. "They apparently represent intentional burials" (Howells 1938, p. 319).
6. Holocene.
7. "Some stone tools and bone beads" originally divided by the workmen are now reunited with the original collection; 3 projectile points are of common late prehistoric type.
8. ———
9. $F = 0.376\%$; bone originally divorced from documented finds and now reunited, $F = 0.286\%$.
10. ———
11. Torrington 1. Male, early middle age: cranium, mandible (f).
    2. Female, young: calotte (f).
    3. Female, middle aged: cranium, mandible (f).
    4. Subadult: petrous portion of the temporals, the malars, and a portion of the mandible with a few teeth.
12. Howells, W.W. (1938). Crania from Wyoming resembling "Minnesota Man." *Am. Antiq.* 3(4):pp. 318–326.
13. Howells (1938).
14. Agogino, G.A., and Galloway, E. (1963). The skulls from Torrington, Wyoming: a re-evaluation. *Am. Antiq.* 29:106–109. The Torrington skeletal material owes its suspected antiquity to its osteologic similarity to Minnesota Man. A recent study of the Torrington remains based on laboratory analysis and grave artifacts, indicates that these burials are of late prehistoric age.
15. Howells (1938).
16. ———
17. American Museum of Natural History, New York City, New York.
18. ———

TRANQUILLITY

1. Tranquillity.
2. Site 4-Fre-48 is located 4 km NE of Tranquillity, California, in the central San Joaquin Valley, approximately 300 m WNW of B.M. 173, Jameson Quadrangle.
3. Investigated by Gordon W. Hewes in 1939; excavated by Linton Satterthwaite in 1944.
4. Imbedded in and on Fresno hardpan and in loam topsoil at depths that varied up to 76 cm; at some points the soil had eroded to the hardpan owing to the action of slough water, which also originally exposed the site. Hewes, G.W. (1946). Early Man in California and the Tranquillity Site. *Am. Antiq.* 11:209–215.
5. Articulated, semiflexed burials; some miscellaneous bones scattered by erosion.
6. Late Pleistocene/Early Holocene.
7. ———
8. *Camelops hesternus* (fossil camel), *Equus occidentalis* (extinct horse), *Bison antiquus figginsi* (bison), *Cervus nannocles* (tule elk), *antilocapra americana* (american antelope), *Canis sp.* (dog or coyote), *Urocyon cineroargenteus* (gray fox), *Taxidea taxis* (badger), *Lepus californicus* (jackrabbit), *Scrapanus sp.* (mole), *Thomomys bottae* (pocket gopher) (Hewes 1946).
9. Bones heavily mineralized with collophane $Ca_3(PO_4)_2$ (Hewes 1946).

   Human remains: 6071, F = 0.185%; 6072A, F = 0.156%; 6072B, F = 0.102%; 6073, F = 0.208%; 6075, F = 0.136%, Ca = 34.1%, P = 17.0%, CO_3 = 6.12%, C = 0.70%, N = 0.053%, H_2O = 2.17%.

   Associated fauna: 51570, F = 0.228%; 61635, F = 0.210%; 61979, F = 0.236%;, 64948, F = 0.128%.

   ". . . . the two lots of bones must be considered as practically identical in chemical constitution" Heizer, R.F., and Cook, S.F., 1952). Fluorine and other chemical tests of some North American Human and Fossil Bones. *Am. J. Phys. Anthrop.,* 10:289–304.

   UCLA-1623: Human femur, F = 0.11%, N = 0.04%. Human 1 metatarsal, F = 0.12%, N = 0.06%. Human r humerus, F = 0.98%, N = 0.05%.
10. 2,550 ±60 B.P. (UCLA-1623).

11. Tranquillity 1. (UCMA 6071) adult, male: partial calvaria (dolichocephalic); incomplete postcranial skeleton.
    2. (UCMA 6072) adult, male: incomplete calvaria; postcranial skeleton (f).
    3. (UCMA 6464) adult, female: calvaria (barely dolichocephalic); postcranial skeleton (f).
    4. (UCMA 6073) adult, female: incomplete calvaria (mesocephalic); postcranial skeleton (f).
    5. (UM) young adult female: calvaria (dolichocephalic); postcranial skeleton (f).
    6. (UM B-181-184) adult, male: calvaria (dolichocephalic); postcranial skeleton (f).
    7. (UCMA 6075) young adult, male?: cranium (dolichocephalic).
    8. (UCMA 6074) subadult: mandible and long bones (f).
    9. (UCMA 6075a) middle-aged female: occiput and base of skull.
    10. Miscellaneous skeletal fragments.
12. Hewes (1941).
13. Angel, J.L. (1966). Early skeletons from Tranquillity, California. *Smithsonian Contrib. Anthropol.*, 2:1–19.
14. Berger, R., Protsch, R., Reynolds, R., Rozaire, C., and Sackett, J.R. (1971). New Radiocarbon Dates based on bone collagen of California paleo-Indians. Contributions of the University of California Archaeological Research Facility. No. 12, pp. 43–49. Berkeley.
15. Angel (1966).
16. Hewes, H.W. (1941) "Reconnaissance of the central San Joaquin Valley" *Am. Antiq.* 7:123–133.
    Wormington, H.M. (1957). *Ancient Man in North America*. 4th ed. (Denver Museum of Natural History., Pop. Sci., No. 4), p. 231. Denver.
    Heizer, R.F. (1952), "A review of problems in the antiquity of man in California. In Symposium on the antiquity of man in California. University of Calif. Archaeol. Survey Rept., Berkeley. 16:3–17.
17. University of California Museum of Anthropology, Berkeley, California.
18. ———

TRENTON

1. Trenton.
2. Within the limits of the city of Trenton, New Jersey.
3. In December 1899, by Mr. E. Volk; investigated by F.W. Putnam.
4. In a railroad cut 2.286 m ($7\frac{1}{2}$ ft) below the surface, in sand, under an apparently undisturbed deposit of glacial gravel.
5. Not a burial.
6. Terminal Pleistocene.
7. "The specimen bears evidence of what appear to be traces of human workmanship" (Hrdlicka 1907).
8. ———
9. ———
10. ———
11. Trenton 1. Human femur, from a little below the trochanters.
12. Putnam, F.W. (1890?). Paper presented before section H of the American Association for the Advancement of Science, winter meeting of the section, at New Haven; there is no published report of this meeting. Yale University, New Haven, Connecticut.
13. F.W. Putnam (manuscript in preparation in 1907).
14. ———
15. Putnam manuscript (1907).
16. Hrdlicka, Ales (1907). *Skeletal Remains Suggesting or Attributed to Early Man in North America*. Bulletin 33. Washington, D.C.: *Bureau of American Ethnology*.
17. ———
18. ———

UTAH LAKE

1. Utah Lake.
2. On the E shore of Utah Lake, about 1.6 km N of the mouth of the Provo River, Utah.
3. By 3 boys, Arlo and James Nuttall and Elwin Bunnell, in July, 1933; investigated by George N. Hansen (1933-1934).
4. Under 23 cm of lake bottom mud (Utah Lake is a remnant fresh water lake of ancient Lake Bonneville of Pleistocene age), at a level 10 cm below the lake's natural outlet, exposing a wide, gently gradient, lake bottom area.
5. ———
6. Unknown.
7. ———
8. ———
9. ———
10. ———
11. Utah Lake 1. "Utah Lake Skull Cap": calvarium (dolichocephalic).
12. Hansen, George H. (1934). Utah Lake skull cap. *Am. Anthropol.* 36:431–433.
13. Hansen (1934): ". . . approaches the upper range of Neanderthal possibilities."
14. ———
15. Hansen (1934).
16. ———
17. Department of Geology, Brigham Young University, Provo, Utah.
18. ———

VERO BEACH

1. Vero II.
2. Open site on N edge of town of Vero Beach at upper end of former Van Valkenburg Creek and 2.4 km (1.5 miles) from Indian River. 27°45′N, 80°25′W. Florida.
3. E.H. Sellards and associates, February, April, and June 1916.
4. Alluvial sand intermixed with vegetable material at contact between the Van Valkenburg and Melbourne formations. Sellards, E.H. (1916). On the discovery of fossil human remains in Florida in association with extinct vertebrates, *Am. J. Sci.*, Ser. 4, 42: 1–62.
    Sellards, E.H., Chamberlin, R.T., Vaughan, T.W., Hrdlicka, A., May, O.P. and MacCurdy, G.G. (1917). Symposium on the age and relations of the fossil human remains at Vero, Florida. *J. Geol.* 25:1–62. Stratigraphic context questioned.
    Rouse, I. (1951). A survey of Indian River archaeology. *Yale Univ. Publ. Anthropol.* 44:171–189.
5. Probably a burial from erosional surface cutting across Melbourne formation, disturbed by well digging (Rouse 1951).
6. Late Pleistocene, Melbourne stage. Sellards, E.H. (1952). *Early Man in America: A study in prehistory.* Austin: University of Texas Press. Holocene, post-Melbourne (Rouse 1951).
7. Flint spalls, 1 polished bone point, 3 pins, 1 bone awl. (Sellards, E.H. 1916). Probably pre-ceramic culture. Rouse, I. (1950). Vero and Melbourne Man: A cultural and chronological interpretation. *Trans. N.Y. Acad. Sci.* 12:220–225. Rouse (1951).
8. *Megalonyx jeffersoni* (giant ground sloth), *Equus occidentalis* (extinct horse), *Mammonteus americanus (M. primigenius?)* (mammoth) (Sellards, E.H. 1916). Contemporaneity with man questionable. Chamberlin, R.T. (1917). *In* Sellards, E.H. *et al.* (1917) pp. 35–39.
9. ———
10. ———
11. Vero I. Female: calotte (ff), mandibula (f), lt. I², costae (ff), rt. scapula (f), lt. humerus (f), lt. radius (f), 2 unlae (f), metacarpale (f), 2 phalanges, lt. os coxae (ff), 2 femora (ff), rt. tibia (f), lt. fibula (f), rt. talus, rt. cuneiform III, 3 metatarsalia (ff).

12. E.H. Sellards (1916).
13. Stewart, T.D. (1946). A re-examination of the fossil human skeletal remains from Melbourne, Florida, with further data on the Vero skull. *Smithsonian Misc. Coll.* 106:1–28.
14. Plhak, M. (1975). "Chronologie und Morphologie der frühesten fossilen Homini-den Amerikas." Masters Thesis, University of Frankfurt.
15. Stewart (1946).
16. Sellards, E.H. (1937) The Vero finds in the light of present knowledge. *In* Mac-Curdy, G.D. (ed.) (1937). *Early Man.* Philadelphia: J.B. Lippincott Co. pp. 193–210. Rouse (1950).

    Rouse, I. (1952). The age of the Melbourne Interval. *Bull. Texas Archaeol. Paleontol. Soc.* 23:293–299.

    Wormington, M. (1957). *Ancient Man in North America* (4th ed.) Denver: pp. 226–227.
17. Florida Geological Survey, Tallahassee, Florida.
18. United States National Museum, Washington, D.C.

WORCHESTER COUNTY

1. Worchester County.
2. On the Farm of William U. Maynard in Northborough, near the Shrewsbury line, Worchester County, Massachusetts.
3. W.H. Raymenton, October 1885; investigated by F.W. Putnam (1885).
4. On the blue clay covering the bottom of an old basin or pond, beneath 15 cm of peat (Putnam 1885).
5. Natural deposition.
6. Undetermined.
7. ———
8. *Mastodon americanus* (mastodon) (apparently in the same soil horizon, but under 20 cm of peat).
9. ———
10. ———
11. Worchester County 1. Skull and mandible.
12. Putnam, F.W. (1885). Man and the mastodon. *Science*, 2d. Ser., 6(143):375–376.
13. ———
14. ———
15. ———
16. ———
17. Peabody Museum, Harvard University, Cambridge, Massachusetts.
18. ———

YUHA (SALTON SEA)

1. Yuha Desert (Yuha Man).
2. Section 19, Coyote Wells Quadrangle, in the Yuha Desert in Imperial County, California. 32°41'N, 115°53'30''W. Elevation 450 m above sea level.
3. W.M. Childers in 1970; excavated by W.M. Childers and E. Burton (1970). Fall of 1971 by Department of Archaeology of the Imperial Valley College.
4. Below cairn formed by boulders and coarse-grained alluvium, 40 cm below top of cairn. Rock cairn and sediments are part of alluvial deposits well cemented in a calcium carbonate caliche.
5. One burial; interment on back, with the head to the north, turned to the left, looking east. Lower limbs below the knee were retracted in a semiflexed position.
6. Middle to Late Pleistocene conglomerate of local origin (Canebrake Formation) overlies silts and fine sands of Pleistocene age (Colorado Delta, Palm Spring Formation) on top of marine sands of Pliocene age (Imperial Formation) on top of Miocene rocks and pre-Cretaceous metamorphic rocks. The burial belongs to the uppermost layer of Middle to Late Pleistocene age.
7. Two unifaced artifacts and several flakes. No proof as to intentional interment of artifacts. They are beaked scrapers or cores of ''ridge-back'' variety, 12.5 by 7.5 by 7 cm, and 10 by 5 by 7 cm. Black metabasalt.
8. ———
9. Yuha I. Tibia: $F = 1.2\%$, $N = 0.68\%$, $U = 16$ ppm.
   Skull: $F = 1.4\%$, $N = 0.73\%$, $U = 14$ ppm.
10. A1: $21,500 \pm 1,000$ B.P. (^{14}C dating).
    Based on caliche coating of bone fragments, sample 104 Geochron Laboratories Cambridge Massachusetts, GX 2674.
    A2: $22, 125 \pm 400$ B.P. (^{14}C dating) (UCLA-2600 = UCLA-1854, $19,000 \pm 3,000$ B.P. on basis of ^{230}Th dating of bones caliche coating of underside of exposed cairn boulders, sample Fra-103 and UCLA-1854.*

---

*The UCLA laboratory No. UCLA-2600 reported in Bischoff *et al*. (1976) should be changed to UCLA-1854.

A3: Based on samples from caliches in Yuha formation from 3 to 10 miles from
     burial.

     24,000 + 2,000, − 1,000 B.P.   Sample 401 (^{230}Th)
     27,000 B.P.   Sample 601 (^{230}Th)
     30,000 + 3,000, − 1,000 B.P.   Sample 801 (^{230}Th)
     32,000 B.P.   Sample 402 (^{230}Th)

11. Virtually complete skeleton. Part of the pelvic region, tibiae, and foot bones
     missing (*Homo sapiens americanus*). Non-Mongoloid (Protsch 1978). Ursprung
     und Migration der fossilen Subspezies des ''anatomisch modernen Menschen'' des
     Oberen Pleistozäns. *Archäologisches Korrespondenzblatt*. Mainz: Verlag Philipp
     von Zabern. Vol. 4, in press.

12. Childers, W.M. (1974). Preliminary report on the Yuha burial, California. *An-*
     thropol. J. Canada, 12:2–9.

13. ———

14. ———

15. Childers (1974).

16. Bischoff, J.L., Mirriam, R., Childers, W.M., and Protsch, R. (1976). Antiquity of
     man in America indicated by radiometric dates on the Yuha burial site. *Nature*
     (London) 261:128–129.

17. San Diego Museum of Man, San Diego, California.

18. ———

CANADA

TABER

1. Taber (Stalker Site).
2. East bank of Oldman River 3 miles N of Taber, Alberta, Canada, 49°50'N, 112°05'W.
3. Field party of A. MacS. Stalker in 1962.
4. Unit H: alluvium underlying glacial till believed to be left by classic Wisconsin ice advance. Stalker, A. MacS. (1969). Geology and age of the early man site at Taber, Alberta. *Am. Antiq.* 34:425–429.
5. ———
6. Wisconsin.
7. ———
8. ———
9. ———
10. A4: 30,000 B.P. on basis of dating of similar till at corresponding section (Stalker 1969). Oakley, K.P. (1964). Frameworks for Dating Fossil Man. Weidenfeld and Nicolson, London, pp. 7–8.
11. Taber 1. Infant about 2 years: frontale (ff), parietalia (f), occipitale, maxilla (ff), mandible (f), vertebrae (3), rt. clavicula, scapula (f), costae (2), femur (f).
12. Langston, W., and Oschinsky, L. (1963). Notes on Taber "Early Man Site." *Anthropologica*, n.s., 5:147–150.
13. Langston and Oschinsky (1963).
14. ———
15. ———
16. Stalker, A. MacS. (1962). *Surficial Geology, Lethbridge (East Half) Alberta*. Ottawa: Geological Survey of Canada. Map 41, 1962. Stalker, A. MacS. (1963). *Quaternary Stratigraphy in Southern Alberta*. Paper 62-34. Ottawa: *Geologist Survey of Canada*. Wormington, H.M., and Forbis, R.G. (1965). An introduction to the archaeology of Alberta, Canada. *Denver Museum of Natural History Proceedings No. 11,* Denver.
17. National Museum of Canada, Ottawa. N.M.C. No. XV-C5.
18. ———

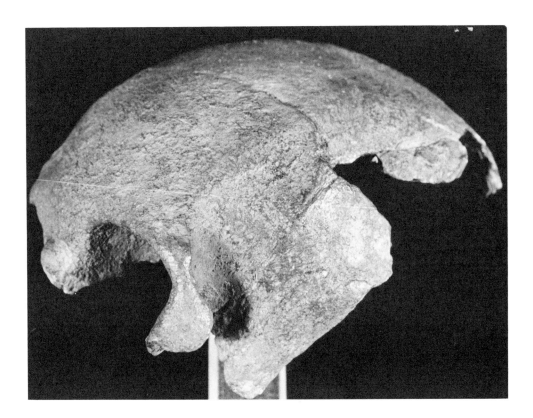

Plate 2. Laguna Beach Woman

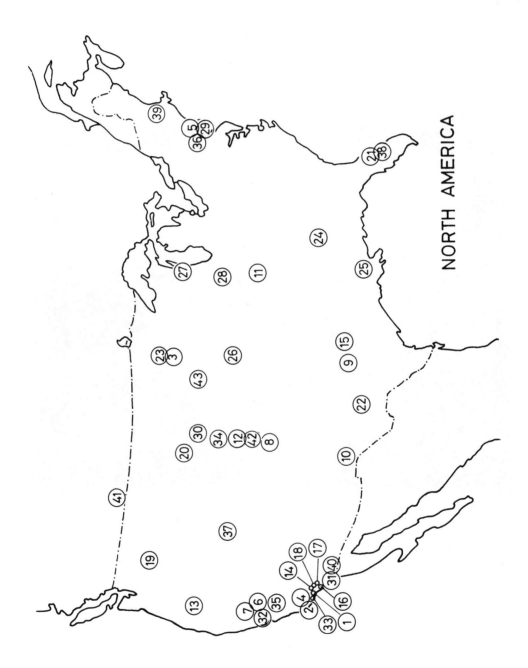

KEY TO MAP LOCATIONS

1. Angeles Mesa (Haverty Man)
2. Arlington Springs
3. Browns Valley
4. Buena Vista Lake
5. Burlington County
6. Calaveras
7. Capay
8. Cimarron River (Folsom Man)
9. Clear Fork (J.C. Putnam)
10. Conkling Cavern
11. Faulkner
12. Gordon Creek
13. Kawumkan Springs
14. La Brea (Rancho)
15. Lagow Sand Pit
16. Laguna Beach (Woman)
17. Little Sycamore
18. Los Angeles Man (Woman)
19. Marmes
20. McKean
21. Melbourne
22. Midland
23. Minnesota
24. Mulberry Creek
25. Natchez
26. Nebraska "Loess Man" (Gilder Mound)
27. Renier
28. Rock Bluff
29. Riverview Cemetary
30. Sauk Valley
31. Scripps Estates (La Jolla) (San Diego Man)
32. Stanford
33. Tecolote Point
34. Torrington
35. Tranquillity
36. Trenton
37. Utah Lake
38. Vero Beach
39. Worchester County
40. Yuha (Salton Sea)
41. Taber
42. Linger
43. Medicine Crow

Index

Abalone, black 36, 62

Abalone, red 36, 62

Academy of Natural Science of Philadelphia 50, 51

adolescent 28, 54

adult 11, 12, 14, 16, 19, 28, 32, 33, 36, 37, 39, 42, 43, 46, 48, 50, 52, 53, 57, 59, 61, 62, 66

Agate Basin Complex 26

Agogino 35, 64

Albritton, C. 45

alluvial 12, 14, 16, 21, 22, 26, 33, 37, 69, 72, 77

American Museum of Natural History 64

amino acid dating 59, 60

ancient 19

Anderson, D.C. 26

Angel, J.L. 66

Angeles Mesa, Haverty Man 11

Antelope (Tetrameryx) 31

Antevs, E. 47

Antilocapra americana 39, 65

Archaic 14, 25, 63

Archaic (Early) 26, 47, 54

Archidiscodon imperator 37

Arlington Springs 12

astragalus 57

avifauna 27, 29

Bada, J.L. 60

badger 65

Bannell, E. 68

Barbour, E.H. 52, 53

Bass, W.M. 42

Baumhoff, M. 19

Berger, R. 12, 23, 29, 33, 37, 61, 62, 66

Bertrand, K. 54

Bielicki, T. 39, 40

Bien, G.S. 60

Bischoff, J.L. 73

bison 31, 41, 45, 50, 65

Bison antiquus figginsi 31, 45, 50, 65

bison, large-horned 50

blackbird, yellow-headed 27

bone pin 43

Bowden, A.O. 37

brachycephalic 52

Breternitz, D.A. 26

Brevard County 43

Broecker, W.S. 12

Brown County 54

Browns Valley 13, 42, 57

Bryan, K. 47, 57

Bryan, W.A. 11, 23, 57

Buena Vista Lake 14

Buffalo County 42

burial 13, 19, 22, 23, 25, 27, 31, 33, 36, 42, 45, 48, 49, 54, 59, 62, 64, 65, 67, 72, 73

Burlington County 16

Burton, E. 72

Calaveras 17

Calaveras County 17

Californian mule deer 36

calottes 23, 32, 64, 69

calvaria 28, 35, 37, 41, 45, 46, 52, 56, 61, 66, 68

Camelops 31, 32

Camelops hesternus 23, 31, 65

Canebrake formation 72

Canis 65

Capay 19, 20

Capromeryx 45

Cariacus macrotis 36

Carter, B.F. 60

cavia 47

Cervus canadensis 26, 39

Cervus elaphus 31, 39

Cervus nannocles 65

Cessman, L.S. 27, 28

Chamberlin, R.T. 69

chamoecephalic 16, 56

Champlain 55

child 36, 53

Childers, W.M. 72, 73

chipped point 14

Cimarron River 21

clavicula 43, 46, 57, 77

Clear Fork 22

Clemens, T. 37, 38

Clovis horizon 27

Cobbey Canyon 19

Colbert County 48

condor 29

Conkling Cavern 23, 24

Conkling, R.P. 23

Coogan, A. 42

Cook, S.F. 19, 37, 43, 65

cormorant 36

costae 39, 69, 77

cowry shells 36

cranium 13, 22, 26, 28, 29, 33, 39, 42, 43, 47, 52, 55, 57, 64

Crook County 41

Crook, W.W. 31, 32

cuneiform 69

Cypraea sp. 36

Daggett, F.S. 29

Daugherty, R.D. 39, 40

deer 31, 39

de Jarnett, D.L. 49

Deneid 41

dentes 13

Denver Museum of Natural History 21, 51, 66, 77

Department of Anthropology, University of Minnesota 47, 58

Department of Anthropology, University of Toronto, Canada 35

Department of Geology, Brigham Young University 68

de Pradenne, A.V. 17
Dickson, M.W. 50
Division of Physical Anthropology, United States National Museum 22
dolichocephalic 13, 19, 21, 52, 55, 66, 68
dolichocranic 35, 49
Dowson, J. 35
ducks 27
Duncan point 42
Dune Dweller 62

Early Culture 19
Early Lauderdale Focus 48
Eden-Scottsbluff 54
elephant, extinct 37
Enhydra lutris 36
Equus 23, 43, 45
Equus occidentalis 23, 29, 43, 45, 50, 65, 69
Ereptodon 50

Faulkner 25
Faulkner focus 25
femur 12, 21, 22, 28, 32, 53, 57, 67, 69, 77
fibula 21, 22, 26, 32, 43, 53, 57, 69
Figging, J.D. 21
Florida Geological Survey 70
Fluted point 27, 42
Folsom age 35
Folsom Man 21
Forbis, R.G. 77
Foster, J.R. 48
Franklin County 39
Frey, D.G. 39
frontal 23, 28, 35, 39, 52, 53, 77
Fryxell, R. 39, 40
F,U,N—see microanalysis

Galloway, E. 64
gastropod mollusks 59
Gazin, C.L. 43
giant ground sloth 23, 43, 50, 69
Gidley, J.W. 43
Gila 22, 27
Gilder, R.F. 52
Glacial 55, 67, 77
Glasscock, K. 45

Gordon Creek 26
gravel pit 13, 57
gray fox 65
grebe 36
ground sloth 23
guinea pigs 47
Gustafson, C. 39

Haliotis chacherodii 36, 62
Haliotis rufescens 36, 62
Hansen, G.N. 68
Harradine, F. 19, 20
Harris, R.K. 31, 32
Heizer, R.F. 19, 29, 37, 38, 43, 61, 65, 66
Henry, J. 55
Hewes, G.W. 65, 66
Holmes, W.H. 17
Holocene 14, 19, 25, 27, 36, 41, 47, 48, 54, 59, 62, 64, 69
Holocene (Early) 11, 13, 21, 23, 26, 42, 43, 61, 65
Homo nosusmundus sp. nov. 21
Horney, A.G. 33, 62
Howells, W.W. 31, 64
Hrdlicka, A. 16, 17, 21, 29, 38, 44, 47, 52, 53, 55, 56, 67, 69
Hubbs 59, 60
humerus 22, 23, 26, 28, 43, 53, 57, 65, 69
Huntington, C.S. 52

ilium 28
Imperial County 72
Indianoid 42
infant 77
innominates 22, 41, 57
Irving, W.N. 42
Irwin, C. 54
Irwin, H.T. 13, 39

jackrabbit 65
jaw 52
Jenks, A.E. 13, 47, 57, 58
Jensen, H. 13
Judkins Formation 45
J.W. Goethe University, Frankfurt, Germany 34, 38

Kawumkan Springs 27, 28
Keel, B.C. 39
Kollman, J. 55
Krieger, A.D. 45
Kroeber, A.L. 29

Laboratory of Anthropology, Washington State University 40
La Brea 29, 30
Lagow Sand Pit 31, 32
Laguna Beach 33
La Jolla—see Scripps Estates, San Diego Man
La Jolla Culture 59
lambdoid 28
Langston, W. 77
Larimer County 26
Laughlin, W.S. 28
Leidy, T. 51
Leighton, M.M. 22
leptorrhine 13
Lepus 45
Lepus californicus 65
Levertt, F. 13
Libby, W.F. 23, 33, 54, 61, 62
Linger 35
Little Sycamore 36
loam (zamora) 19
Loess Man—see Nebraska Man
Loomis, F.B. 43
Lopatin, I.A. 37, 38
Los Angeles 37
Los Angeles County Museum of Natural History 11, 30, 34, 38
Lyell, C.E. 50
Lyman, C. 54

MacClintock, P. 47
MacCurdy, G.G. 44, 69, 70
MacNeish, R.S. 25
Mammonteus americanus 31, 43, 69
Mammonteus primigenius 31, 43, 69
Mammuthus 31, 32, 43, 45, 69
mandibula 13, 21, 22, 23, 26, 28, 29, 32, 39, 43, 47, 53, 54, 55, 57, 64, 66, 69, 71, 77
Marmes 39, 40
Marmes, R.J. 39
Marriner, E.H. 33

Mason, R.J. 54
Massac County 25
Mastodon americanus 50, 71
mastoid 28
Mattison 17
maxilla 28, 77
May, O.P. 69
McCann, F.T. 57
McCown, T.D. 61
McKean, K. 41
McKinley, J.C. 21
Medicine Crow 42
Megalonyx jeffersoni 23, 43, 50, 69
Meighan, C.W. 63
Meigs, A.A. 55
Melbourne 43, 44, 69, 70
Melbourne Stage 69
Merriam, J.C. 11, 29
mesocephalic 42, 52, 66
mesocranic 42, 62
metacarpal 43, 69
metatarsal 57, 65, 69
microanalysis 12, 17, 19, 23, 32, 37, 43, 45, 50, 61, 64, 65, 72
micromammalia 26, 39
Middle Culture 19
Midland 45, 46
Midland Complex 45
Minnesota 47, 64
Mirriam, R. 73
molar 64
mole 65
Mollusca 11, 12, 39, 62
mollusk (gastropod) 59
mollusk (pelecypod) 59
Moriarty, J.C. 59, 60
Morris, W. 52
Mulberry Creek 48, 49
mule deer 36
Mulloy, W.B. 41
Museum of Anthropology, University of California, Berkeley 20, 66
Museum of Anthropology, University of Michigan, Ann Arbor 25
Museum of New Mexico 45, 46
Museum of Southern Methodist University 32
mussels 39, 48
Mylodon 50

Mylodon halani 50
Mytilus californianus 59
Mytilus californicus 33

Natchez 50
National Museum of Canada 77
Nattal, J.A. 68
Nebraska Man 52, 53
Neff, G.F. 39
Nelville Public Museum 54
Neumann—see Deneid
Newman, M.T. 49
Nothrotherium 23
Nothrotherium shastense 23

Oak Grove 36
Oakley, K.P. 12, 31, 32, 45
Odocoileus hemionus 36
Olivella 36, 62
Olivia flammulata 36, 62
Olson, E.A. 12
Oregon State Museum of Anthropology 28
Orr, P.C. 12, 62
orthocranial 42
os calcis 53
os coxae 26, 50, 69
os occipitale 23, 28, 39, 52, 77
Oschinsky, L. 77
Otter-trail County 47

palatine 54
Paleo-Indian 13, 14, 26, 29, 37, 45
Paleo-Indian Institute, Eastern New Mexico University 24
parietal 28, 35, 39, 52
parietalia 23, 39, 77
Parker, F.T. 52
patella 59
Patterson, D. 35
Peabody Museum, Harvard University, Cambridge, Massachusetts 16, 17, 26, 56, 71
Pelecanus sp. 36
pelvis 21, 28, 50, 53, 73
Peromyscus 12
Phalacrocorax aristotelis 36
Phalacrocorax pygmaeus 36
phalanges 53, 69
phalanges manus 46

Pindale Stage (mid) 39
Pisces 39, 59
pit burial 26
Plainview point 42
Pleistocene (Late) 12, 23, 33, 37, 42, 45, 50, 65, 69, 72
Pleistocene (Terminal) 12, 13, 22, 26, 31, 32, 57, 67
Plhak, M. 29, 33, 37, 44, 46, 70
Pliocene 17, 19, 72
Plum-pudding 14
pocket gopher 65
Podiceps auritus 36
Podiceps cristatus 36
Podiceps griseigena 36
postcranial 12, 29, 39, 42, 54, 57, 66
pronghorn antelope, extinct 31, 45
Protsch, R.R.R. 12, 23, 29, 33, 37, 66, 73
Pullman (Washington State University) 39, 40
Putnam, F.W. 67, 71
Putnam, J.C. 22

Quimby, G.I. 50

radii 22, 48, 53, 57
radiocarbon 12, 23, 26, 29, 33, 37, 39, 59, 60, 61, 72
radius 23, 26, 69
ramus 28, 32, 39, 53
Ray, C.N. 22
Raymenton, W.H. 71
Renier 54
Reptilia 47
Retzek, H. 57
Reynolds, R. 29, 33, 37, 66
Rhinoceros antiquitatis 17
ribs 26, 32, 48, 53, 57
Richards, W.A. 31, 50
Richmond, G.M. 39
Riddel, F.A. 33, 40
ridge-back 72
Riverview Cemetary 56
Rixon, A.E. 45
Roberts, Fr. H.H. 21, 22
Rock Bluff 55
Rodentia 26, 47
Rodgers, M.J. 59
Rogers, D.B. 36, 62

Rouse, I. 43, 69, 70
Rozaire, C. 29, 33, 37, 66

Sackett, J.R. 29, 33, 37, 66
sacrum 53
Salmonidae 27
Salton Sea—see Yuha
San Diego County 59
San Diego Man 59
San Diego Museum of Man 59, 60, 73
San Diego Museum of Natural History 60
San Joaquin Valley 14, 65, 66
Santa Barbara Museum of Natural History 12, 36, 62, 63
Santa Monica Quadrangle 11
Santa Rosa Island 12, 62
Sardenson, F.W. 13
Satterthwaite, L. 65
Sauk Valley 57
scapula 21, 22, 53, 69, 77
Scharbaur Interval 45
Schmidt, E. 50, 55
Schroeder, R.A. 60
Scrapanus sp. 65
Scripps Estate 59, 60
sea otter 36
Sellards, E.H. 32, 69, 70
Sellards Llano Culture 27
Seymour, B. 61
Shuler, E.W. 31, 32
Shumway, G. 59, 60
Signal Butte I 41
Singleton, C.P. 43
Siphateles 27
skeletal 14, 17, 23, 25, 43, 46, 47, 49, 50, 54, 57, 64, 66, 70
skull 16, 17, 19, 21, 25, 27, 28, 29, 32, 35, 37, 42, 43, 52, 55, 61, 64, 66, 68, 70, 71, 72
skull cache 41
Snow, C.E. 49
stalagmite 17
Stalker, A. Mac S.
Stalker site—see Taber
Stanford 61

Stanford Geological Museum, Stanford University 61
Stary, P.F. 47
Stephenson, R.L. 42
Stewart, T.D. 14, 22, 23, 24, 33, 41, 43, 44, 45, 50, 70
Stock, Chester 11, 29, 30
subadult 14, 28, 52, 53, 62, 64, 66
Suess, H.E. 60
superciliary arches 35
supraorbital margins 35
Swedlund, A.C. 26

Taber 77
talus 69
Tanulapolama sp. 23
Taxidea taxis 65
Tecolote Point 62
temporalis 23, 28, 64
Teratornis merriami 29
Tetrameryx sp. 31
Thomomys bottae 65
Thwaites, F.T. 54
tibia 21, 22, 26, 32, 43, 53, 57, 69, 72
Tod County 57
Tompkins, E. 57
Torrington 64
Tranquillity 65, 66
Trenton 67
Trivela stultorum 62
Trivia californiana 62
Tulamni 14
Tulaminu 14
tule elk 65

ulna 22, 23, 26, 43, 48, 53, 57, 69
United States National Museum, Washington, D.C. 15, 22, 44, 55, 70
United States National Museum, Washington, Anthropology Division 39, 40, 41, 44
University of California, Museum of Anthropology, Berkeley 20, 66
University of Colorado, Museum 26

University of Kentucky 49
University of Nebraska 53
University of Southern California, Los Angeles 36, 37
Urocyon cineroargenteus 65
Utah Lake 68

Valkenburg Van, Formation 43, 69
Vaughan, T.W. 69
Ventura County 36
Vero 43, 69, 70
vertebrae 21, 22, 26, 27, 39, 53, 77
Volk, E. 56, 67

Walker, E.F. 14
Wallace, J.W. 11, 36, 38
Ward, H.B. 53
Warren, C.N. 59, 60
Washington, H.H. 29
Webb, W.S. 49
Wedel, W.F. 14, 15
Weis, P.L. 39
Wendorf, F. 45, 46
Wertzbaugh, H. 26
Whitney, J.D. 17
Wilford, L.A. 57, 58
Willis, B. 61
Wilson, T. 18, 50
Wilson, W.H. 33, 34
Wisconsin 22, 39, 59, 77
Wisconsin (Late) 12, 33, 52, 57
Worchester County 71
Wormington, H.M. 51, 54, 61, 66, 70, 77
Wright, H.E., Jr. 39

Xanthocephalus xanthocephalus 27

Yerington, W.F. 79
Yolo County 19, 20
Yuha 72, 73